# SO YOU WANT TO BE A PREACHER?

## Tutoring Trainees for Ministry

By

Vernon D. Lloyd

# So You Want to be a Preacher?
## Tutoring Trainee for Ministry

Copyright 2016
by
Vernon D. Lloyd

Vernon Lloyd Ministries

# IN MEMORY OF:

## Minister Sherilynn O'Neal

# DEDICATION PAGE

Pastor. Dan James
Pastor. Douglas Stanley
Pastor Antawin Hambrick-Lloyd
Pastor Jamie Paulk
Pastor Shawn Curtis
Rev. Otis Dixon
Pastor Ricky Stanley
Pastor Kendrick Smith
Deacon Arby Lagroon
Sister Reda Mae Brown
Evangelist Barbara Martin
Sister Amanda Bouyer
Sister Guynelle Ellington

Thank you for the privilege of being able to share in your development and being witness to the blessings you all have become.

# TABLE OF CONTENTS

# ACKNOWLEGEMENTS

This book is special for many reasons. First, it is a compilation book. It is a meshing of things that I have learned from my pastor along other ministers who have mentored me in my ministry and things I have been able to share with those I have been able to mentor along the way.

Second, it is special because it enables me to refine and revisit so many things that I need to remember and leave in a form that may well outlast my mortality. It gives me the opportunity to share with those I have never met and may never meet except upon these pages.

Finally, it gives me the opportunity to release the former and make room for the new. Every releasing of a word or impartation gives room for the fresh to enter and for great filling to occur. I am grateful for this in ways words cannot speak.

I desire to express great appreciation for several people who have made my ministry a better thing than I could ever make it alone. A great debt shall never be able to be re-paid to my pastor Dr. Roy A. Allen. Casual conversations with him were life classed that you cannot learn in bible college or seminary. Special appreciation is also extended to Reverend Alfred Reid, Reverend Roosevelt Carter, Dr. L. Perry McNeal, Reverend M.D. Dumas, Dr. Troy Allen. Dr. Fred Samson III, Dr. Lamar Holley and Dr. Jack Key for investing uniquely in my formation and cultivation in ministry.

I am forever grateful for the churches that I have been granted the privilege to pastor and those I have been afforded the opportunities to minister in other capacities in for your patience and support over the years. You have borne my errors, tutored me in many things and been patient with me in my learning. I thank my true critics who critiqued me lovingly to improve and increase me as well as those who have opposed me and taught me that all the best relationships do no start easy.

May God bless you as you thumb through these pages and find nourishment and encouragement that will enhance you in your ministerial quest.

Vern

# INTRODUCTION

For a long time, I have pondered the whole preaching enterprise. It used to seem so simple and I admit to being presumptuous of my ability to do it. It seemed tedious and without thankfulness. I saw it as something that men of slow desire to succeed in anything else would aspire to or that those of astoundingly high moral character would be perfectly suited to.

A little while later I changed perspective going in an almost entirely different direction. I saw the role as highly charismatic and open to those with good voices and oratorical skills that could turn a congregation out like performers did at concerts. I saw people who were respected and honored. I saw those who were celebrated and seemed to have little worry and had the whole "Christian life" wrapped around their fingers.

As I grew I recognized my extremities. I had gone too far left and then too far right and the real thing came to me. In the summer of 1979 while walking down Yellowstone Street in my hometown of Detroit, Michigan I heard an unusual voice. It was not highly audible but range clearly in my spirit. I stopped but saw no one but I knew I was not alone. I continued to hear this voice for some days and began to question myself. Surely I was not having some sort of religious experience. Surely the Lord could not have been…wait…Not me! I asked, "Is God trying to get my attention?"

I ignored it for about a month when I noticed that there was no escaping it. It terrified me to think that I would fall into a category of people that I had great admiration for but never wanted to be counted as one of them. I prayed and sought clarity in my spirit. I asked the question, "Who is ever going to believe this?"

I confronted myself went to my pastor and shared my feelings with him. With tears in my eyes I said, "Pastor, I have something to tell you. I have been called to preach." He calmly leaned back in his chair and looked at me with understanding eyes and said, "I have expected you."

I was astonished at what he said and knew that I was in a grip that I could not escape now. But what do preachers do besides preach? What do they need to understand? How do they act? What are the consequences? Can I live to the standard? I am terrified to stand before an audience so how am I going to do this? I still have some sins I have not given up all the way so how am I going to manage this? These were just a few questions. There were many more.

I wanted to be a preacher but I needed a lot of help. I was fortunate to have a pastor who was caring, giving and wise. He mentored me and raised me very well and subjected me to other great preachers and teachers who could teach me things that he did not know as well as they did.

He walked me through practical lessons and challenged me to understand the box I had to grow up in and how to think outside the box to take my ministry to another level. He taught me how to embrace opportunity, handle success and deal with failure. He held me accountable to the Lord, himself, the congregation and community. I was humbled and made to be proud. I learned God wanted a "Me": that had to be grown out of much toil.

It has been 37 years since I began this journey and the lessons have been learned daily. There are things that may seem to come easy that yet cost me because I have learned them on the base level and now operate on a higher perfecting level. They did not and still do not come easy. Often I have sincere well-meaning people come to me saying how much they really want to preach and minister the word of God. I hear the words, "I cannot wait to preach or I cannot wait to pastor" and I say, "Hold on and let me talk to you before you get too much fire in your desire and not enough knowledge in your head."

I have had the opportunity to not only learn from others but also to mentor a number of diverse ministers. I have been privileged to stand with those who have answered the call to preach and done so in wonderful ways.

This book is a compilation of wisdom given to me and wisdom that has come from me to enable those who minister to have some tips and training on how to handle all sorts of issues as they go forth in ministry. It provided guidelines and tools. It gives examples of how to approach issues and allows the preacher to cultivate a heart for God's people. It is a conversation with all who want to minister God's word. It is not for those seeking deep theological engagement but for those who want an honest engagement about ministry and what it takes to be who you are called to be.

Read these pages as tutorial and use them as a workbook. I pray that as I share with you that you will find courage and stability for the job. I offer myself and my experience to you.

# LETTER OF ENCOURAGEMENT TO FRIENDS AND SELF: TRANSPARENCY

Pursue what is in you. Take time for you and the person waiting to breathe in you. I want to encourage you. Believe in you dream and let others share in it to. This is probably the most personal I will ever be on Facebook. I pray that my transparency will help someone else as well as reveal my own need to express myself. When I was a young man I was always introverted. I held a lot within. I knew what I wanted and yet I did not take the time to believe in what I wanted to do and be. I believed in everyone else's dreams and made great strides to help make them happen. I feared my own talent and aspirations. I was afraid to look deep within myself and see myself for who I really was. Myself concept hid me from my true self and I would talk to me in secret but never share with others.

I am a grown man and I have made many strides. I have come to a place that I was when I was a young man. I asked myself...Where do you go from here? The LORD has called me to a life based on a step by step journey and it is the most blessed/difficult thing I have ever done. I cannot manipulate it, change it or guess at it. I cannot question it because I do not know what IT is. I live every day on faith.

I took inventory of what I want to do. My pastor asked me today..."Where are you headed to Lloyd? What will you do?" I sat and thought. The question was not "What can you do?" It was "What will you do?" I paused and declared "I will teach the scriptures. I will engage in training and Christian education wherever I can. I will lead workshops where I can and preach the gospel where I can. I love the ministry. It is my calling and most desired thing to do. I will write books and speak on what I write. I will write poetry and plays because I love the beauty of poetry and drama. I will help people and build them up. I begin with the seed of my own self. That is all I have but it is a good seed. I will live and minister in such a way that I will make a living and I will live dreams that I never have given myself a chance to. I do not have anything tangibly that I speak of but I believe in God. I believe He will open the right doors and sow me." Abraham believed God and it was counted to him as righteousness..."

I finally said it. I heard myself and despite what I did not see I felt in my belly that God would honor what I said. After 55 years I said it all. I went to the mirror and repeated it to myself later. A friend asked me who overheard me "why are you putting yourself through this? What do you hope to accomplish?" I said I am living what I have been preaching. When my journey is complete I will be able to say with a renewed confidence that God will take care of you. I will be able to say that he can make a way out of no way. I can tell others to follow the Lord if you feel Him leading you a particular way because He is worthy of trust. I can say that I have found Him faithful in all things. I can say to you that he will take you through whatever you need to go through to get you where He wants you. I told Him that I will learn the path to an unrealized destiny. I smiled and said AMEN.

I write this letter to you to tell you to trust Him. No matter the circumstances or seeming lack...TRUST HIM! Move beyond your obvious things and understand that the declarations of his mouth are certain. You are special. Look deep within and see the person He will show you if you open your eyes. Believe in your own ability and what it can become when God uses it to His glory. Give Him the offering of your own self. I share this with you at 55 because some of you are younger and need to understand that He is the God of your younger years. Some of you are older...know that He is still God in your latter years.

Pray for me and for each other. The kingdom needs us all. From this point until the day I die there is a purpose I have to fulfill. There are lives I need to touch and bless and mine needs to be touched and blessed by others. I will meet you on the road. I will be packing...WITH THE GIFTS HE GAVE ME... If I can help or be a blessing to you I will be here. I know it is a long letter. If you are still here I thank you for taking the time to read it. Now go out and do YOU to the MAX!

# SAY WHAT?

The day that you announce that you have a call to ministry of the word of God and take that call seriously, you enter an arena of life that will mark you forever. You become responsible to care for, defend and feed God's people with that which He gives you. Your most representative and essential tools become your cross, your bible, your hymnal, your voice, your prayer and your faith. So you really want to be a preacher? Let's see if you really understand what you are asking for.

# SO YOU WANT TO BE A PREACHER?

Before you jump know what you are jumping into. Do not accept the cheap and inauthentic road to ministry. It is a blessed call but requires much more than is often shared. The philosophy of "just open your Bible and mouth and let the Lord speak through you" is horribly misguiding and presumptuous." If you enter this call every word you share has the potential of leading to life or even death. So you want to be a preacher? Here is SOME of what it takes.

You must be saved

You must be grounded

You must be called to preach

You must be humble

You be submissive

You must begin under someone credible

You do not dictate the time that your ministry happens.

You must demonstrate a commitment to ministry before being allowed to preach.

You must develop a disciplined spiritual life.

You must be taught what preaching is and is not

You must learn to meditate

You must to better communicate in prayer

You must learn to hear God as a preacher

You must be taught to preach

You must learn how to write your preaching

You must learn to preach

You must learn to preach to yourself

You must learn how to address a congregation

You must practice preaching

You must grow what you are learning

You must be willing to be mentored

You must understand the ramifications of being licensed to preach.

You must understand that preachers made too fast seldom last.

ALSO UNDERSTAND THIS....the made is ready only to preach. Pastoring is an entirely different course. The MADE preacher must learn in like manner where he/she fits in the five-fold sense

# WISDOM POINTS

*Knowledge will be important as you embark on your journey and will never cease to be important. The preacher who places no premium on it shall soon dry up and out. Ignorance no matter how well masked has no place in it. However, the preacher must seek to be wise and keep an ear open for it. It will keep you when you are not certain how you have been kept. Take a few points from the vault before going further here.*

The call to preach does not begin with a thunderous call from the sky but a disruptive urging of the spirit that summons you to a higher place.

The first step in accepting the call to preach is to listen to what God is saying. How you begin to do this is prepares you for a lifetime of listening.

A call to preach does not mean you are ready to preach.

Behind the desk is the first place the preacher should go.

The best thing that the aspiring preacher may do is to shadow the seasoned one.

Be easy on the flaws of preachers who have gone before you for you have not yet been tried.

Preaching is not the mere dispensing of biblical words and phrases but it is encountering the REAL God that you might engage His very real people.

Preaching is not easy work for those who do it well.
Learn the lesson of the text before you launch any preaching endeavor.

Every aspiring preacher ought to know how to remember the

pastor's sermon, repeat the pastor's sermon, reflect on the pastor's sermon; re-write the pastor's sermon, re-preach the pastor's sermon.

Sit before a wise preacher and you shall become a wise one.

The Pulpit must never be mounted with Bible alone.

Peaching is a laborious task that many never know takes so much out of you.

Let the young preacher first learn to listen,

Let the young preacher learn to life what is heard.

Let the young preacher learn to look at the older for example and wisdom.

Let the young preacher learn how to look at the scriptures more deeply.

Let the young preacher learn how to outline the messages of others.

Let the young preacher learn to be more observant than spoken.

Let the young preacher learn offer few opinions until the lessons of being a preacher have been learned.

"Speak Lord" ...the preacher's essential request before ever attempting any preaching endeavor.

Let the older preacher impart unto the younger one that which gives them a head start in church and ministry

Let the seasoned preacher share with the fresh of his own seasoning.

Style matters little in preaching if fabric is poor

When the preacher speaks is should be because God has spoken.

You are not ready to preach until you may say, "Thus says the Lord…"

The preacher is an instrument by which humanity hears the voice of God.

You will not preach most or your best of sermons on Sunday.

Preaching involves agonizing over others and taking on their burdens and pains because the heart of God is in you for them. It is the uncomfortable but very profitable privilege that comes in serving God.

Some of what you feel are your best sermons shall prove to be your worst and what you feel was worst will prove most beneficial.

Preaching will not come easy for you cannot do it without Him and what He works in you also works on you.

Everyone you become involved with shall be affected by your ministry therefore be as honest as possible about who you are and what you have been called to do.

Do not live presumptuously nor seek to take on battles as you begin that were meant for more seasoned warriors.

There are a host of tiered demons waiting for you as you enter this arena.

Do not let cheering and supportive congregations fool you. Your greatest battles will not be won before them.

Preaching requires that you sit where others sit and feel what others feel before you can sufficiently minister to them.

Style points matter little in preaching. It is far better to say a great word in a basic manner than to say nothing in the most fascinating one.

The footsteps you follow determine the path that you begin to take and validate your experience. In these footsteps  you are established. The preacher who has few footsteps that have been followed is not worthy of following for that preacher has presumed a journey that he has not known and has not learned what it takes to be who he is nor how to lead others.

Samuel cannot stand before Israel until he has served before Eli.

Your first sermon shall be your most difficult but easiest sermon. The difficulty shall be with your preparation and the reality that what you say you may be held accountable for in eternity.  The easy part shall be that most people will come to cheer you the first time not to hear you.  Seldom will this happen again.

Preaching requires much time alone and before God.  The busy soul has little time to be faithful to it and to do it well.

In silence we hear best and alone we commune best with God.

The best sermon never goes forth before a congregation first but before the mirror.

You are not ready to speak best before others until you have endured the agony of preaching to your own self.

The little opened bible will not support one who seeks to open it only before a crowd.

The one who stands before people professing the word that is shared is of God is responsible for every ear that opened itself to hear.

Preach where you are and not where you aspire to be one day.

Let no false expression be used to add decor to your message.

Insure that your life validates the level of the word you preach.

# PREPARING FOR A FIRST SERMON:

## 8 things necessary

### Thought

You cannot be strong in preaching if you are not willing to think. You must take intentional time to think both great and small thoughts. You must intentionally expand your mind, faith and imagination. Do not be led to feel that you may just stand up and release the Word of God without thinking. Such is the practice of the presumptuous who later become classified as fools.

### Truth

All thought is not truth. Measure out what is genuine truth and what is your thinking. As with many foods, all parts are not edible but most is usable in one way. Truth is found and grown in thought. You must be a seeker of it that you might both preach and practice it.

### Theme

Every message must be going somewhere. There must be a focus on something that controls where you are going. This is made known in the theme. Zero in on the area or topic you are going to talk about. Present it in a memorable manner so that the congregation might remember it and what you intend to say.

### Text

Every message must have an authoritative base. What that does not mean is that you can find something you want to talk about and then put a scripture reference on it that you have no plan to expound upon, say what you want and call it a message. That is what is called "proof-texting" or poor exegetical counterfeiting. The message is not about the text but emerges from the text. See what is in in and you will know what you may take out of it.

### Techniques

You may study a text for preaching several ways to get the best from it. You will not approach it the same way every time. Several techniques in approaching the text are devotionally, biographically, topically and exegetically. A notebook will be your best friend for it will retain things that you would otherwise forget and enable you to build upon what you have extracted utilizing these techniques. Do not rush to know for it takes time and if you do you will find that you cheat yourself of what was truly available to you.

## Tools

To get at the deepest treasures of the Word you will need more than your bible. The bible is your primary tool for it is the Word of God but you will need to dig and invest in quality tools such as study bibles. Concordances, bible dictionaries, bible almanacs, bible handbooks, devotionals, histories, books on customs, language tools and commentaries. Truth, like oil, may be discovered in shallower places but to release the best of it requires that you have the tools to reach the depths.

## Toil

You must spend much time before God otherwise what you say may be right but not authorized for you to say. You labor in the scriptures. There is no reward or commendation for laziness. You must be willing to Read, Re-read. Write what you read, Reflect, record your reflections, Research, Re-Write, retain what you learn. You will live in a perpetual state of perfecting what initially appeared to be perfect knowledge. You will spend much time in prayer and in meditation aside from study. These two disciplines will make your preaching and ministry more robust. Your eye and ear will sharpen therefore your words shall have a power that is not possible without the authority and unction of the Holy Spirit.

## Treasure

Do not walk away from the quiet place with low regard for your time there. Do not drop or waste what you extract from it. Secure it in the containers of your heart, your mind, your soul and your journal. Keep company with them regularly and see them as investments the Lord has made in you that shall never cease to bear interest.

# FIRST SERMON PREPARATION II

The aspiring preacher shall not just choose something to preach but will learn what will continue to be re-learned as one goes along: preaching takes prayer and preparation. The following will be things that need to be done to begin and be continued for you to become the most effective preacher.

1. Ask God what to say
2. Seek God for text and theme
3. Share your message idea with your pastor
4. Get approval to preach it before the congregation
5. Learn to let the text speak to you
6. Write what it speaks to you
7. Study the text
8. Take excellent notes on what you study
9. Prepare the study in lesson form
10. Write the message in manuscript form
11. Seek audience with your pastor
12. Preach the message to yourself
13. Submit the message to your pastor for critique
14. Receive assessment and make corrections
15. Re-submit manuscript
16. Preach the message before your pastor alone
17. Make corrections
18. Re-preach message to pastor
19. Seek new hearing
20. Make corrections
21. Preach before a committee of four or more
22. Receive helpful suggestions
23. Make corrections
24. Re-submit manuscript for approval
25. Preach first public sermon

# FIRST SERMON PLAN

The first sermon is not an audition but an introduction to the world of preaching. You do not come raw but you are inexperienced in it. Do not approach the task with low regard or with the sense that you are free to do as you will. Pastors provide guidance for you and in following it shall you become successful. Here is a preaching plan for the first sermon that will prove helpful as you begin and continue your initial journey.

You will learn to be disciplined. Your first sermon shall be thirty well spent minutes at a maximum. You shall adhere to this as a good steward. You shall be critiqued by a panel of five of your peers for your presentation before the people. This is not to question your calling or to give overwhelming support but to evaluate your readiness and to go before God's people corporately. Your budget for time shall be as follows:

**Five minutes for the introduction**
Your introduction shall emerge from the context of the message and flow into the text. You shall not build a disconnected introduction nor shall it be filled with testimony of how you were called to preach. This is an initial sermon which means you have prepared for this moment. Now you must own it. An introduction is like the porch to a house. Upon it you meet the people and tell them what you are about to tell them. The yard is the contest in which the house is set. Tell them what you are going to tell them here so that when you get into the message they know what they are looking for.

**Twenty minutes for the body of the sermon**
This is the main portion of your message and it emerges from the text. When you were on the porch (Introduction) you told the congregation what you were going to tell them or show them in the message. Stay on point. You will see so many other things as you are sharing but stay with what you said you would share. Wandering about will lead to confusion and your message will lose clarity. Also, do not let the response of the congregation or lack thereof to

cause you to lose focus. Stay with the message you promised to deliver. You have twenty minutes to make it clear.

**Five minutes for the closing of the sermon**
The first rule here is that you shall not take the opportunity to show or exit in an overly dramatic fashion. Are we quenching the spirit? No! We are providing discipline. Closing the message is important because it solidifies what you have done. On the porch you told them what you would tell them. In the body of the message you tell them what you told them you would tell them on the porch. The closing of the sermon is your telling them that you told them what you said you would tell them on the porch. Your exiting the message does not mean there is no more to say on the matter but it is a wrapping up of the message. At this point thou shalt not whoop, holler, squall, fall out, sing a song or anything else. You shall complete the word God gave you, say thank you and sit down.

# PREACHING PERMIT

The preaching permit shall be given to the preacher who successfully completes the preacher preparation program and the delivery of the first sermon. It is restrictive in that the preacher is permitted to preach but only in one's home church or if certain special or emergency circumstances should arise with the permission of the pastor and under the supervision of another ordained pastor. It is an in-house authorization that is upgraded at the time of full licensing.

The permit is given to anyone sanctioned to handle the word of God under the supervision of the pastor only. The preacher's road test was the first sermon but now the time to learn how to navigate in unexpected, sometimes unfavorable and diverse ministerial capacities must be learned and one sermon shall not provide that kind of knowledge nor is the preacher able to function as he/she should before different congregational settings.

Adherence to this permit and its requirements as well as restrictions are a good testimony and further the new preacher in the ministry. Failure to do so revokes the privilege and expels the aspirant from the preacher training program.

# THINGS EVERY PREACHER MUST UNDERSTAND

...and no church should entrust a pulpit to anyone who cannot answer and understand the following:

What it means to be called to preach
What the step is after answering the call
How you learn to preach
What is expected in a first sermon
Where you learn to preach
How you prepare to preach
How to mentor preaching
What preaching is
When to preach
What a trial sermon is
Who determines when you are ready to preach
Why licensing to preach necessary
What a license implies
Who licenses the preacher and why
When a license should be given
What to do when asked to preach
How ready should I be to preach
What a text is
What a theme is
What the word "homiletic" means
What the word "hermeneutics" mean
How long should the sermon be
What some do's and do nots of preaching are
How to grow in preaching
The different types of preaching
Difference between preaching and ministering

# WEEKLY PREACHING PATH

The preacher in training must be attentive to ministry and give to it in every setting. Preparation shall be held at a premium in the growth of the individual. Pastors provide the model for what they desire their aspiring ministers to become therefore they must be attentive to what they teach by example. Preachers do not first learn preaching by preaching. They learn preaching by studying, mentoring and example. As the best players on a sports team must practice and prepare before playing so must the preacher do this each week and not just when he/she is asked to preach. Here is a suggested weekly path to discipline and prepare the aspiring preacher.

1. The preacher is responsible to maintain a preaching journal that includes outlines of the Sunday Sermon and commentary that the preacher has on it that has been gleaned from studying it.

2. A scripture and devotional thought that has been gathered. The thought should be no longer than one paragraph.

3. Notes from a particular book that you have been assigned for the month demonstrating your commitment to preparation.

4. Bible Study notes

5. Prayer Journal

The pastor holds these ministers accountable by regularly checking these journals and showing himself willing to give supportive attention to the growth of the preacher. Journals are issued quarterly (13 weeks) and are to be maintained for future reference and development also. The one -year licensing program shall require four complete journals to before the preacher qualifies to enter it.

Before moving on remember…

The preacher is called a "workman" therefore the path that is required to be walked out to require work.

The aspiring preacher should not expect to set the pace in preparation. Follow the leader.

Mistakes will be plenty but do not be afraid to make them for they are stair steps to perfection.

# WHEN IN THE PULPIT

Limit your conversation with others in it.

Dress for what the occasion requires

Come with bible, journal and pen at all times

Be the example for how the congregation should   worship.

Be prepared for whatever assignment given

Do only what you are asked to do or what you are assigned to do. Take no liberties on your own.

There shall be no wearing of liturgical apparel that has not been approved by the pastor.

Flashy dress and distracting jewelry are not permitted while preaching or ministering in any capacity from the pulpit.

No conversation with others in the pews while in the pulpit.  All needed conversation in this manner shall be done prior to service or through the ushers.

Be courteous and alert at all times

No eating at any time is to be done while serving in pulpit.

Do not linger in pulpit after service but step down to greet others and fellowship.

# VISITING OTHER CHURCHES

When entering the church do not report to the pastor's office or pulpit without being invited.

Sit in the congregation without drawing attention to yourself.

Introduce yourself without title.

When visiting with your pastor receive your assignment from him.

Remember at all times that you represent your church and pastor no matter where you are.

Do nothing away that you would not do at home.

Be gracious and thankful at all times.

Do not linger in the pulpit or in confidential areas before or after service.

When business matters of a congregation are being handled be sure to excuse yourself even if approved to remain.

# LICENSING THE PREACHER

*Licenses to preach should never be given until the preacher is prepared for the road. When they are the church and the pastor take responsibility publicly for what that preacher both says and does. It is not the mere issuing of a paper to a person to practice the art of preaching but a sanction that this person is ready to speak and minister the word of God into the lives of others on behalf of church that issues this license.*

Note the following:

Licensing the preacher makes the pastor and the congregation responsible for every word he utters on their behalf.

The preaching license entitles the preacher to preach at home and is a testament that of skills obtained to do so.

Licensed preachers qualify to enter the ordination program.

Licensed preachers are not given the privileges to do all things granted with ordination.

Licensing the preacher does not entitle the preacher to go where he/she desires without consent or communication.

No license should be given that does not meet a criteria of requirements.

# LICENSING REQUIREMENTS

Must exemplify a lifestyle conducive to preaching ministry.

Must be an active member of the church.

Must be committed to prayer and study.

Must maintain a weekly preaching journal detailing Sunday messages of pastor's messages.

Must be able to expound on 18 articles of faith

Must have sat under pastor a minimum of 6 months in preparation

Must be faithful in worship and bible study and diligent in preacher preparation work.

Must be able to construct an expository sermon

Must be able to conduct a full service

Must submit a paper to pastor on what preaching is and what it means to me.

Must pass licensing examination.

No license will be given before 1 year of training.

Upon reception of license one may enter ordination program.

# ADVICE TO YOUNG MINISTERS

*CLARIFICATION: When I say YOUNG MINISTERS that is not meant to refer to chronologically young ministers but to those who are young in the ministry. I pray that this advice might be strengthening to them as them move towards a more mature and gratifying ministry*

Advice to Young Ministers I: Your calling does not move you from common to elite status. You have not entered a level of superior ministerial identity that does not permit you to fellowship with the "ordinary." You are not due a higher title or respect. You are the same person in a different role. You may still learn from your previous teachers and should never forget that no matter how much you learn from here they gave you your foundation. Grow up right in the Lord. Fools step in footprints made by themselves. Always know that you are not sufficient alone. Arrogance compels us to see ourselves with our eyes closed and to measure ourselves with no real measure.

Advice to Young Ministers II: Preaching is learned. It does not come just because you are called. It requires time, study, reading, writing, questioning, digging, conviction, practice, audience awareness, sensitivity, wisdom, temperament, devotion, insight, perseverance, courage, determination, understanding passion time in the presence of God, tears, and the ability to see one's self among the very people he/she preaches to. Preaching is learned and if you never do learn it you shall never truly do it.

Advice to Young Ministers III: Study before you are called upon. Preparation is not for the event but a manner of life. The effective minister takes the time to sharpen skills and load the arsenal before called upon to release and sere. That minister does not waste time with the frivolous when it is time for the faithful. Open your book and heart to the word and the will of God. Make your daily life a perpetual visitation with God and engaging one with your own self. When called upon for rich ministering you shall not have to be ashamed and others can receive what you were made to give

Advice to Young Ministers IV: Do not be so anxious to build new things that you do not take time to understand what has come forward from yesterday. Do not forget where you came from nor where you are going. There are some excellent mentors to help you and you cannot make old things disappear. They mother your present vision. Do not despise tradition for you are a part of what was moving into what it is and what shall be. Be your own person but do not forget the person that you are

Advice to Young Ministers V: You are human. Never forget that. The call to minister does not remove you from your essential nature. You are not given a cape and cast into the realm of super hero. You have human feelings, desires, needs and emotions. You can rise strongly and fail miserably. You get tired and you do not have all the answers. When offered a seat on the pedestal refuse it. Stand on the wall when it is your time and know how to steal away when necessary. Make your announcement of your humanity to all who develop their expectations of you. God can greatly use you as the wonderful human being that you are.

Advice to Young Ministers VI: Take care of your body. Sometimes in the midst of our quest to be strong spiritually we fail to understand "we have this treasure in earthen vessels." We fail to embrace the need for physical maintenance. Exercise, sleep, eat well, reduce stress, laugh, dance, love much and take time for yourself. Dress up and present yourself as the person you desire to be seen. In your quest to be all that you desire to be take care of YOU! The vessel must be well maintained it is to deliver the goods that God has provided for it to deliver

Advice to Young Ministers VII: Be considerate of the faults and flaws of others in ministry that you meet. The gospel is a high calling that is administered by those striving to live it. When you are privy to the struggles of others as they declare the gospel it is for you to help them by striving with and helping. You are called to administer support while you admonish each other. The flaws are your privilege to view because of where you are allowed in their lives. Remember that as you are looking at them so are they looking at you. Be sensitive. Be kind. Be trustworthy. Be supportive.

Advice to Young Ministers VIII: When it comes to marriage do not look for a first lady or a first gentleman. Look for a spouse. The church does not need a husband or wife. You do! The call of a pastor or any other person in ministry is the call issued to a person with a gifting. When you see your essential self as your calling you have missed the uniqueness in your ministry. When you find the person that fits you the two of you now made ONE can go anywhere together. You cleave and dwell with and in each other. You serve together and are happy not because of the church you are at but because of who you are together. Do not seek to conform to the expectations of any person or the collective membership. You may change churches one day. Make sure they do not have to keep being someone they may not be to fit the next place you may be sent to.

Advice to Young Ministers IX: Build your own circle. Surround yourself with people from three categories. (1) Find like-minded people that are on your level. You need the fellowship and the growth together. Learn how to experience things together and how to work through some of the same issues. (2) Find people who are on a higher level. When you have no one smarter or wiser than you then your growth potential is limited. Draw from their advice and guidance. Ask questions and walk with them in dimensions that you have not experienced so you will get a preview of what to expect. (3) Find someone you can help or mentor. Teach them as you learn and give them as you receive. Remember that those who are ahead of you will one day move on and you will succeed them. Train someone to take your place when you move up and there will be strength in the ranks.

Advice to Young Ministers X: The way to look like a minister is not based on the clothes that you wear but the character that you exhibit. You light ought to shine and your behavior ought to reflect the true personality of Christ. You need not make God look good with the finest suits, dresses, shoes and jewelry. It is good to be well dressed but that is not what makes you. Clothe yourself in the finer garments of character and spirit and you shall always make a classy presentation

Advice to Young Ministers XI: Be patient with others and earn the confidence in leading. Just because you have a title does not mean you are good at what you do yet. You may be prepared but you have not yet been tried. Until your bio reads that you have survived a few wars, survived a few wounds, have a few scars and come through a few trials others are hesitant to follow you through the most critical things in life. You may know some things to be true but not know them experientially. Speak and lead even if they do not first trust you. It is okay. We all must earn it. Be patient in receiving it then thank them for giving you the opportunity

Advice to Young Ministers XII: Preaching events are not like suits for new occasions. When you are asked to preach you do not always have to come up with something new. You do not have try to get something unique for every occasion. What God begins in one setting He will use you to complete in another. Let the Word grow rich in you. Because you have preached a message once does not mean it is finished. One sermon point grows to a full sermon. One sub-point grows to a full point and one devotional thought becomes a full teaching. As you grow so shall your preaching grow. Let the word of God grow in you.

Advice to Young Ministers XIII: Study when you do not have to preach or minister. The blessing in ministry is being fueled when there is no occasion. God wants you for relationship more than engagements. If you should hit a dry spell in preaching and ministering you shall not feel like you are wasting time or energy because the relationship with God will be stronger. You are at your best with God when you are in private. Fill up before you have to hit the road

Advice to Young Ministers XIV: Do not become encumbered by accolades nor discouraged by criticism. The ultimate critique on ministry lies with God and not with who applauds you or does not.

Positive critique and appreciation may be helpful but they are not the ultimate determinations on your ministry. Listen to what the Spirit says and consider sincerely and in prayer what you hear from others

Advice to Young Ministers XV: Learn it before you do it. Imitation is easy. Learning takes time. The synthetic flower looks just like the original one. It is as beautiful and serves as beautiful appearance however it has no fragrance. It has no root. It can grow no deeper or higher. It gives nothing and can receive little from anything or anyone else. I cannot reproduce. It is sufficient as long as you ask nothing of it and leave it alone. Do you get the message? Take time to learn.

Advice to Young Ministers XVI: Look to the real side of ministry and take your eyes off the seeming glitz. It is not easy or simple and the dents and scratches you see in many that you look down upon have come from engagement, war and necessary mileage. Pastoring is blessed tough work because you minister to many people at once. You preach to them on Sunday. You minister Monday through Saturday. If you have no time to demonstrate your declaration before them, you lose authority and credibility to declare it. You give because you have been entrusted and if you cannot handle hardship and rejection without whining and complaining you are in the wrong place and call. Pour out because you have allowed Him to pour in. You are called to be a servant not a star therefore does not seek to shine as such. Be God's preacher on His terms. Anything else is counterfeiting and worth no more than what you give yourself and others pay you to do. Shall we continue?

# PREACHER/PREACHING NUGGETS

There is a calling to preach that includes a calling to ministry. Find your place in it and learn to labor.

Your gifting will determine the places that God desires to facilitate growth in you.

The call to preach does not mean that one stands around looking for the next engagement but perpetually seeks to sharpen skills and grow in the ministry until mature and strong.

Preaching reproduces itself. The sermon that had three points becomes a three sermons and the three sermons with three more points becomes a series. Never write off what you have only seen the first layer in.

Preaching resounds and it echoes therefore do not be afraid when you hear voices speaking to you when no one is presence. It is God speaking back to you what you declared for Him before others.

There is no deeper spirituality given to the one who can go the pulpit without a manuscript. The prime purpose in going is not to demonstrate one's own self-sufficiency. Preaching is dependent behavior and whatever means you are given to deliver it, by all means do so.

There is no power in showmanship. Responses from congregations do not determine whether you are preaching or not. Listen to the one telling you what to say and know that if you delivered that then you have succeeded.

There is a spirit of worship and the Spirit in worship. Be governed by the latter and not the last.

# PASTORAL DO'S AND DONT'S ON PREACHERS

1.  Do be attentive to those that minister the word in your church.

2.  Do be aware of the quality of teaching that goes forth in your church.

3.  Establish a standard for teachers and preachers in your church.

4.  Do have a method for receiving preachers into calling and then training.

5.  Do lend your support to anyone that you receive into the preaching ministry.

6.  Do accept them and become the father in ministry they will need.

7.  Do prepare them diligently for the preaching ministry.

8.  Do seek to build other mentors into their lives to be support beyond yourself and to give character and ministerial validity to who they are and what they do.

9.  Do provide resources and opportunities for them to learn.

10. Do hold them accountable to a disciplined life

11. Do not direct a person into ministry based on your opinion and not their sense of calling.

12. Do not extend the opportunity to the ministry to one scarcely in the faith.

13. Do not receive a person's call because they are a friend and do not restrict one based on a personal view you may have of a person.

14. Do not receive a person into preaching ministry who is not biblically sound.

15. Do not accept a person into preaching ministry who cannot follow or support you.

16. Do not expect more of the one you train than you are willing to give.

17. Do not license a person who does not meet the biblical standard established.

18. Do not distribute preaching opportunities as favors.

19. Do not lower the standard of preaching and training if you do not have it. Learn it before you teach that you might develop others.

20. Do support the aspiring preacher before those in the congregation as well as those in the community.

21. Be honest and fair in your assessments of the work of the preacher.

22. Do support the preacher's family and time.

23. Do not contend for time that belongs to the preacher's family as a way of exemplifying loyalty.

24. Do develop the preacher in such a manner that God will be proud He entrusted you with him/her.

# PREACHING DO'S AND DONT'S

Do cultivate a heart and head to preach.

Do spend time listening for God and to God outside the pulpit so you are familiar with His voice in it.

Do write out notes and manuscripts on a regular basis that you might build upon them later.

Do preach to yourself so you can be sensitive to what others hear through you.

Do prepare yourself as much as you prepare your message to preach.

Do understand who you are preaching to so that you may know how to preach so they may hear.

Do understand the engagement before you take it.

Do rest before preaching and be alert to your surroundings and the unction of the Holy Spirit.

Do know your message well and speak with clarity and authority.

Do believe what you say before you say it to others.

Do think through what you are about to say and pray over its potential impact upon others.

Do preach expecting others to render a verdict on what you say.

Do issue an invitation within the service.

Do be mindful of the time that you stand.

Do not mistake motivational speaking for biblical exhortation.

Do not preach at people to make a point that you have been yearning to make.

Do not go to the pulpit unprepared.

Do not preach on what you have not studied or understood.

Do not preach the sermons of others because you were not prepared to preach what God shared with you.

Do not become preacher who does not pray.

Do not use gimmicks in preaching.

Stay away from fanciful titles that create interest but no greater insight to the truth you are sharing.

Do not attack people in preaching.

Do not speak over the heads of the congregant.

Do not insult the intelligence of others by shoddy preparation and living.

Do not become arrogant and non-receptive to the teaching of others who do not hold the same office as you.

Do not feel that you must close every message with a going by Calvary. The invitation is part of what you do but it need not be the tail of every sermon.

Do not try to sing or whoop yourself out of a bad message.

Do not think that preaching gives you a superior standing before others.

Do not forget that preaching is a privilege and an honor. Do it to the glory of God.

# THE FIRST MINISTRY

Never is it the intent of any well-meaning ministry to take priority over the family of the minister in training. It also is not permitted by this church for any minister to use the work of this church as an excuse to underserve his/her family. In such cases, a restructuring of time and responsibilities shall take place and a conference with the family to ensure that it remains intact in all things at all times.

Schedule time for yourself on purpose each week.

Schedule time to spend with your spouse even as you are required to fulfill ministry assignments. Do not make deny your spouse time and quality attention.

Designate time for your children minus church involvement. Keep your promises and dates.

Do not assume excess responsibilities at church to the detriment of your family.

Take care of your physical, mental, spiritual and financial health. Share when you see either one of these areas growing weak. You need not carry things alone.

Give yourself and your family the opportunity to be normal and abandon all suggestions that you must be perfect.

Enjoy your life and ministry. He did not appoint you to misery but to ministry.

# SUPPORTING PREACHERS WHEN THEY PREACH

Be wary of being non-supportive of the ministers who support the church year in and year out. "Muzzle not the ox who treads out the grain." Because they belong to our churches does not mean that we should not be supportive of their ministries and families when they preach for us. Many feel that they should do all things with no compensation if they are part of our church. Preacher maintain your home. What we put into others we shall surely receive in return. Let the following be a model that you may consider using.

## Book Support:
Every preacher needs leaning material therefore let 20% of every honorarium be designated for a book from the local bookstore or national chain. Gift cards may be used to support this giving.

## Spouse/Family Time:
Preaching and ministering take time therefore let 35% of the honorarium be designated to an event for the family.

## Discretionary Support:
The balance of the honorarium is given to the preacher to use however he/she chooses. It is written in a check to the preacher for their personal use and enjoyment as a way of the church saying "thanks for a job well done."

## Time Support
Pastors must recognize that young preachers are their support and legacy. They cannot be allowed to grow wild. They need time support to learn non-pulpit lessons from you. Time support may be exhortational, correctional, instructional or social. The parent in ministry must bestow time upon the son or daughter in ministry that they would upon a child of theirs. They need to learn by example how to live the life of a preacher. They need to learn how to deal with the pressures and day to day issues of the preacher's life from you. Without this they are severely handicapped and vulnerable to things that they would be able otherwise to deal with much easier.

# ORDAINING THE PREACHER

The journey to ordination is not a simple one. It moves the preacher into a deeper ministry or service. Responsibilities are delegated to help him/her learn how to be supportive in current ministry program and how to identify an area or gifting that the Lord has bestowed that the preacher will work at developing to greater lengths.

Many preachers have felt that this is a time of waiting or that this is the period between preaching and someone calling them to pastor but this is not true. Ordination gives the preacher the opportunity to refine the ministry that is possessed and how to conduct ministry in a much greater way. This process is observed by the pastor and church and when the preacher has reached the maturation point that is desired there is the move to ordain or set that person aside.

Pastors do ordination through the church. The prospective candidate has worked under this pastor and when the recommendation is made following a comprehensive training program a catechism takes place that is a public event and reveals to the congregation the readiness of the candidate for ordination.

You will find some practical things in the next few pages that will help you with understanding and developing an ordination program of you own or how to go about preparing for your personal ordination.

# BUILDING A SUPPORT TEAM

The pastor begins the path to ordination by supplying the candidate with a mentor within the church and four well respected pastors outside the local congregation with differing gifts and abilities that may learn from. These individuals will eventually vouch for his preparation, character and quality of work. They shall also serve as the core group to train him. They shall further serve as the essential catechism team at the time that the ordination is set.

A sample team would look something like this:

Pastor
TEAM LEADER
Coordination and Development

The pastor provides overall enhancement and development for the rising preacher. Life skills, family management, personal development, theological development and training in the areas of the catechism. The pastor mobilizes a team of associates who have specialties they can share with the preacher in understanding and in growth. The ordination process shall take 18 months (one year working in 4 primary areas and then 9 months of one specialty area and catechism preparation. The 9- month stint shall be done exclusively at how with the one-year program being broken into four 3 month assignments under the mentorship of both the pastor and another pastor leader. Each assignment shall be made only after the candidate has obtained some fundamental grounding at home and can prove useful in the setting that is being assigned.

**Administration Pastor**
The prospective candidate is assigned a pastor who is able to help him in the area of church administration and understanding how processes work. This experience is outside of what is learned in the local church and gives the preacher a reference to abilities learned to be effective in this area. This pastor allows the candidate to shadow him in different things and teaches skills that may be applied in

ministering to the home church. Different aspects of administration are taught including finance, budgeting, planning and church governance. Objectivity is the goal here and developing credibility in working with other preachers and pastors. These pastors will be different and selected to meet the needs of the ministry of the candidate. They will benefit the candidate and by enhancing skills and the candidate will benefit the prospective pastor by providing an additional support person for 3 months during ordination preparation in his church.

**Evangelism Pastor**
This pastor assists the candidate in working with evangelism. This pastor permits the candidate to work in an intern manner to reach to people in a congregation beyond his own. This pastor has a heart for missions and evangelism. The development of a philosophy of evangelism is done here and the completion of one local mission project is done.

**Teaching Pastor**
Candidate shall work with the assigned pastor to learn to teach in different groups and utilize different techniques. Candidate shall work with pastor in assisting in developing enhancement skills for Sunday School and bible study teachers and learning how to teach in at least two areas that have not been explored. A philosophy of teaching shall be developed here and shared with the pastor.

**Preaching Pastor**
Here the candidate shall receive assistance in developing keener preaching ability and opportunities to preach in clinics with this pastor as well as provide pulpit support on Wednesdays and some Sundays that the preaching pastor requires assistance. Candidate will learn to address a variety of specified themes in each message preached and will be responsible for the writing of one sermon every week to be submitted to the preaching pastor and then on to the candidate's pastor.

When each phase is completed the pastor who has been assigned to the candidate shall evaluate the work and submit the report to both the candidate and the pastor. Successful completion is one of the 7 steps necessary for ordination. The program requires time and sacrifice. It requires discipline and fellowship with fellow pastors with special skills. The circle built will be different for each candidate but the objective will be the same and permit you to build a well- rounded proven candidate.

# SEVEN STEP ORDINATION PROCESS

Ministry Internship I
3 Months
Ministry Assignment _____

Ministry Internship II
3 Months
Ministry Assignment _____

Ministry Internship III
3 Months
Ministry Assignment _____

Ministry Internship IV
3 Months
Ministry Assignment _____

Nine Month Ministry Specialty
9 Months
Ministry Specialty _____
(This is the ministry to which the candidate is ordained

Catechism Training Program
(Written Examination)

Public Examination
(Oral and Public)

# NON-CONSIDERATION

The ordination program is a disciplined one dedicated to making the strongest and best fit persons for ministry. It is not granted lightly for the sake of the person who would step out prematurely and the sake of the church or ministry that would have to carry the responsibility and consequences for such premature actions.

No candidate shall be ordained without completion of the 7 Step process.

No candidate shall determine his or her own ordination time.

No candidate leaving the church without proper transferal process shall maintain license as a minister of this church.

No church shall receive approval from the pastor to ordain any minister if that minister has not adequately served in his/her home church.

No consideration shall be given to any minister coming to the church for ordination who does not have a verifiable license, history and recommendations from viable individuals that have worked with the individual.

Satisfactory evaluations must be obtained in all areas of the ordination process to be granted full ordination.

The ministerial program is not meant to be unduly difficult nor simple to go through. It is designed to build qualitative preachers and leaders who can stand in whatever environment necessary to represent our God and our church. It is not to be entered into lightly and without consideration of the time and spiritual energy that it will take to be successful.

# LAYING ON HANDS

Ordination is of the church in that the preacher shall become a sanctioned authorized minister of the ordaining church with the rights and responsibilities to perform the duties assigned with full confidence and support of the ordained one's abilities.

Ordination speaks of a confidence and trust bestowed upon a person to represent the church and pastor in matters spiritual and otherwise.

Ordination confers upon one the ability to visit prisons and hospitals, preach at different churches, pastor, serve in other ministerial capacities, officiate at weddings, funerals, dedications and other official functions of the church as a sanctioned representative.

Ordination is to a specialty area as designated on the certificate though the preacher may serve in a wide array of capacities.

Ordination is of the pastor for therein lies the one under whom one is authorized to act.

No preacher may be authorized without pastoral support.

Ordination is a conferral of authority to act on the pastor's behalf and in complicity with the governance of the church.

They laying on of hands is to be done by the pastor demonstrating the relationship between the candidate and pastor.

# CAN YOU BELIEVE…?

A young preacher shared with me that he was surprised at the way church people act. I asked him if he was surprised when non-church people are wise, good, kind, true and devoted. He said." No." I asked if he was as critical if others as he is with church folks...he paused. I shared with him: " your folks are church folks and you are church folks. When you classify all negatively and declare that is how we act you teach those growing that this is the norm. Hold your family up even when they let you Down....it is the one you belong to..."

A young preacher said to me "Rev. Lloyd as you enter retirement age do you have any lessons to share with us young preachers." I replied swiftly that I was not entering retirement but just getting started. I lived 20 learning that I knew little about life. Then I lived 20 more trying to straighten out. the first 20. The last 16 I have used what I learned the previous 40 trying to make a great life happen. I have more ....so much more to do.... He looked surprised. I looked excited.

The young preacher said to me that all he needed was a bible and the Holy Ghost to preach. I asked him..."who will teach you the scriptures in your bible? Who will teach you speaking skills? Who will listen to you? Who will you help? Who will let you minister to them? You cannot fix a car with the Holy Ghost and a manual any more than a life unless you participate with others and sufficiently prepare for others to trust you ministering to them.

A young pastor said to me "You need to change your approach. People do not need that "cross stuff," They need inspiration, entertainment, and a compact message. You have too much eternity in your messages and Jesus is but one way to a multiple door eternal place. You need to get with it!" I said to him "you are no preacher or teacher. You are posturing and promoting. If I do what you tell me I am no more than a poor imposter and weak composite of a preacher. My approach to the gospel is my approach to Jesus." The young pastor came to object but I held up my hand and said..."Stop son. Right now only I KNOW how foolishly you are talking.

A young pastor said to me "You need to change your approach. People do not need that "cross stuff," They need inspiration, entertainment, and a compact message. You have too much eternity in your messages and Jesus is but one way to a multiple door eternal place. You need to get with it!" I said to him "you are no preacher or teacher. You are posturing and promoting. If I do what you tell me I am no more than a poor imposter and weak composite of a preacher. My approach to the gospel is my approach to Jesus." The young pastor came to object but I held up my hand and said..."Stop son. Right now only I KNOW how foolishly you are talking.

# PASTORAL MINISTRY

The shepherding of God's people is a glorious yet laborious task filled with blessings as well as great challenges. One must be willing to celebrate births, raise generations, train and delegate, clean up messes, forgive without being asked, understand when things seem senseless, lead through conflict and when opposed, love beyond hurt and become all things God desires of you even when you do not want to be. You must want the growth of God's people more than they can imagine and take them where they will not go otherwise.

# THE ROAD TO ACCEPTING A CALL TO PASTOR:
## Advice to Aspiring Young Preachers

By "young" I am not implying chronological age by ministerial age. It is easy to fantasize the romance of pastoring and miss the shocking realities. It is indeed a glorious call if God has bestowed it upon you. If not take a step back...it is only one of many. Again, maybe I can help someone.

1. If you have never sat under someone and learned some things about pastoring do not seek the office YET.

2. Because you are a good or exciting preacher does not make you ready to pastor.

3. Never seek a pastorate because of the appearance of it. Prayer is the focus for every consideration you will make.

4. In your inquiries always ask the church for a church history. What a church says and emphasizes of itself in writing will tell you much of it in actuality.

5. When you go to preach at an interested church do that and go home. Do not meet with others outside of the ones who officially invited you.

6. Be honest about your knowledge and ability. Do not be shy about your strong areas nor timid about your weak ones.

7. Seek to be engaging and kind.

8. Because a congregation calls you does not mean that God has. Seek close consultation with God.

9. Seek specifics in your conversation and do not volunteer to do for nothing what it will cost you much to do. A preacher who presents himself as cheap will soon be devalued.

10. Discover how solid the prospective church is in the Word. Ask for a copy of the church calendar. They tell what the church focuses its time and attention on.

11. Make sure all references and contact information is current and with complicity of those you have listed.

12. Do not speculate publicly about the church's consideration of you. Let the process work for itself.

13. Learn all that you can about being a prospective pastoral candidate from wiser men who have gone before you. Understand the process as well as the position.

14. Do not accept a call to an extremely divided church. A very narrow margin is often divisive and oppositional. Understand the temperature of the church during this process.

15. See the layout and size of the pastor's study compared to other facilities in the building. You learn much about expectation

16. Never accept a call that causes you to compromise your moral, biblical or ministerial integrity.

# THE CALL TO PASTOR

1. It means a church is entrusting you to lead and care for it.

2. It means that the search for the person to grow with is over.

3. It means that a church has agreed to work towards the vision of God with you.

4. It means that you are to assume the role as chief servant and under shepherd.

5. It means that you stand in a place of authority and honor.

6. It means that you are now responsible for the spiritual nurture and growth of this congregation.

7. It means that you must cultivate nurturing habits and disciplines to minister to your people.

8. It means that you represent not only the people of the church but also the people of the community.

9. It means putting away childish and immature dispositions and practices.

10. It means that confidentiality and truth become more important than ever.

11. It means a call to an elevated study and prayer life.

12. It means there will always be representative of God present.

13. It means that God is counting on you to care for and bless this flock.

14.

# PASTORAL VACANCY ANNOUNCEMENT:
## (Humorous Reality)

The committee told the pastoral candidate "we need a credit report, resume, background check, references, degree, DVD, CD, license, ordination certificate, 5 recommendations, vision. for the church, philosophy of ministry, marriage evaluation, and 10 years' experience pastoring on this level and proof HE can grow the church while performing ALL the expected duties of the church during the day with at best a part time partial staff and over worked volunteers during the day while making himself available to all meetings and auxiliaries led by members who have REAL jobs and have to work for a living.

He must be on call 24/7 and be a true family man putting his family first. He must be married and have a wife who will offer free services and show up whenever he does while dressing and acting in a manner that pleases us just like we want. He must preach powerful sermons that do not last too long and blend with the social/culinary desires of our congregation. He will be paid as the church grows and should not ask for what would be fair in what we are asking him to do. We will not ask of his prayer life, biblical approach and theology, ministry goals, philosophy of pastoring or discipline practiced and do not really care if he does not bother ours.

He is welcome to stay until the head honchos get angry or tired of him. All relocation and travel expenses are on him and his family. All worthy candidates shall be notified after we have thoroughly vetted you and determine your qualification to lead our most worthy congregation. God bless you. Get those resumes in the mail.

# EXPECTATIONS OF MEMBERS AT A NEW CHURCH

When you go to a church the transitions are not going to be idealistically smooth. Just as you will need to make adjustments so shall they have to make adjustments. The office is occupied but there will be a variety of relationships that will be at the beginning. Personal pastoral acceptance takes time and do not let the diverse acceptances cause you to be negative or oppositional to others. When you go to a church you will find at least three categories of members.

1. There will be those who receive you as pastor:
   There will be those who will readily accept you and will work tirelessly to insure whatever your agenda is that it has muscle and protection. They will be your "go to" people and help you settle firmly.

2. There will be those who come to hear you preach
   They are supportive and encouraging but they are not all the way into your pastoral leadership just yet. They will lend a hand but they still have a few reservations. They are on the willing boat but now overly anxious to pull up the anchor. They are attentive and encouraging. They support your preaching and teaching ministry and look, in a positive way, to hold you accountable.

3. There will be those who come because they are members of the church. They are not sold on you and you were not their first or even second choice for pastor but they are loyal to the church fellowship and determined to be an active part of its success. Their attendance has nothing to do with you.

4. Then there are those who did not want you and are not going to support anything you do. They will be critical of all that you do and make their opinions known in clear voices. They do not come to church much and do just enough to stay active on the membership role.

Love them all for love will bring the whole thing together. Those who allow you to pastor them will grow stronger and will support you in even better ways. If you love those who come to hear you preach they may let you pastor them one day. Those who just come to church, if loved, may even listen to you preach and those who do not come to church and critique you all the time may just come to church a little more regularly if you love them and not be so critical.

This is the art of pastoring people. This is the sacrifice and wisdom. You must be willing to assume these roles. Pastoring is not about power and position. It is about Divine privilege to shepherd God's people

# THE ROAD TO CALLING A PASTOR

I have found a great problem that exists in pastoral search committees. Often they are some of the sincerest people that you can ever find but much of the criteria that is utilized would not qualify the Lord Himself to pastor a local church. The first words are "We are seeking the Lord for a Pastor...but He must have THIS, THAT, THE OTHER THING, HAVE THIS, BEEN HERE, NEVER DONE THAT AND BE WILLING TO DO THIS THIS PARTICULAR WAY while having a vision from You Oh Lord!... Let me share a few helpful suggestions.

1. The quest for a pastor is both spiritual and business. Establish realistic criteria that help you address both needs.

2. The Pastor must first be given to the work of God therefore seek understanding of his prayer life, theology, biblical knowledge, teaching ability and weekly discipline.

3. The committee must be willing to seek the person who is honest in assessment of themselves. Leave room for imperfect particularly since these are the type of people who comprise the flock.

4. Do not ask the prospective candidate what the vision for the church is since he has never been part of it. Ask him his vision for ministry. The church should have a vision from the previous administration that gives direction to it and that can be built upon.

5. The Sunday Sermon will not tell you all you need to know of the prospective candidate's preaching ability. Do not devalue it but do not over rate it.

6. Never politicize the process. One may have a favorite but make no deals. You are there to direct the church to make a choice.

7. Communicate things in writing and be willing to yield information to the prospective candidates in the manner that you

desire to receive from them. Transparency on the part of both are vital to the process.

8. Have a biblical description of pastoral duties that is realistic and fair. Synchronize it with scripture and implement with prayer.

9. Do not make the pastor's wife a consideration outside of the relationship that she has with him and the Lord. Your expectations for what the church desires in a "first lady." She is part of him and family. Aside from that should be no job description for her.

10. Be fair in your expectations of the pastor's children. They are not your primary considerations either in the call.

11. Be mindful of what you desire in a leader and let the task be funded adequately to compensate the candidate for his work and insure that it is done well.

12. Be open to God and bathe each move in prayer. The perfect man on Paper may not be the person God has for you. Stay before God during the call process.

13. Have a time limit. It is amazing that many churches take longer to call a pastor for a 300-member church than a nation of 300 million takes to call a president. With God in the process it need not become that exhausting.

These are only suggestions and hopefully they can help you in your understanding of calling a pastor.

# WHAT EVERY PASTOR OUGHT TO KNOW ABOUT BEING CHRISTIAN

1. Jesus loves us but will not force himself upon us. He will call you will not hunt or trap you.

2. Jesus will not save anyone who does not make him Lord in their life. Salvation is not a hustle.

3. Those who receive Jesus as Lord are kept by His blood and power. Not the opinion or judgment of others. ...

4. Sanctification is both positional and practice. it is separation unto the purpose of God and given positionally when we give lives Him and worked out in practice every day.

5. Justification means you and I have obtained not only a love relationship but a lasting one in which by his sacrifice we have been legally set free and covered with His righteousness.

6. We are adopted (given legal standing) as children of God and thereby made heirs of God and joint heirs with Jesus Christ our Lord.

7. Salvation begins now and lasts forever.

8. Prayer is essential to living a faithful, secure, growing, peaceful and prosperous life.

9. Guilt is the Enemy's tactic to keep you from grace.

10. You are part of the body of Christ and if you disconnect from others you become at best disobedient and dysfunctional.

11. You are part of a diverse people therefore you do not get the right to judge them on the basis of who you are. Celebrate and learn from them.

12. You will suffer for His sake in some things but you shall likewise overcome.

13. You shall go with Him when He returns

# WHAT EVERY PASTOR OUGHT TO TEACH ABOUT BEING SAVED

Who saved you
Why you were Saved
How you were Saved
The meaning of being saved
The obligations of being saved.
What it means to make Jesus Lord
If I can lose my salvation?
What about when I do not feel saved?
Why I am baptized
Spirit and Water Baptism
The meaning of grace
The meaning of faith
The meaning of forgiveness
The meaning of confession
The meaning of prayer
The meaning of atonement/propitiation
The meaning of belief
Bearing fruit
Abiding in Christ
Who Jesus is
Who the Holy Spirit is
Who the Father is
What a sinner is
What a saint is
What the cross did and does
What the resurrection did
The benefits of salvation
What happens at death

# WHAT EVERY PASTOR OUGHT TO REQUIRE A MINISTER OF MUSIC TO KNOW

What worship is
What praise is
How to lead into worship
How to enter the presence of God
What ministry is and how to minister
What a hymn is and when to use it
What a spiritual is and when to use it
What a gospel is and when to use it
What an anthem is and when to use it
What a psalm is?
What a choir is
Differences between choirs and ensembles
How to teach choir parts
How to coordinate musicians
How to work cooperatively with musician and choir
How to lead people into the presence of God
What a call to worship is
What the role of a minister of music is
Understanding this role in the scriptures
The relationship between minister of music and pastor
The relationship between minister of music and choir
The relationship of minister of music and church
How to plan a rehearsal
How to extract the biblical/practical meaning from a song
How to coordinate music with the pastor
The difference between Minister of Music and musicians?
How to refer matters to pastor and church
How to generate a music budget

# WHAT EVER PASTOR OUGHT TO KNOW BEFORE APPOINTING DEACONS

How a deacon is chosen

What a deacon is

The biblical standard

Doctrinal level

Christian Experience

Temperament

What the training program is

What the defined responsibilities shall be

What the training program shall embrace

How long training shall be

If wife shall be incorporated as deaconess

Who shall do training

How long the tenure of deacons shall be

The character of the appointee

The gifts of the person

The ministry background

The relationship with the pastor

How deacons fit in worship

How he wants to use them in worship

How deacons fit in administration

Which deacons have administrative gifts

Ordination procedures

Formal ministry assignments

Leadership Capacity

Conflict Resolution skills

When is a deacon ready to be ordained?

# WHAT EVERY PASTOR OUGHT TO KNOW ABOUT TRUSTEES

What the historical basis for trustees is

How trustees relate to the church

How trustees relate to the government

How trustees relate to the bank

Difference between deacons and trustees

Who qualifies to be a trustee

How to work with trustees

How to assign trustees

Trustees and property

# WHAT EVERY PASTOR OUGHT TO KNOW ABOUT MANAGING THE PULPIT

The pastor is the steward of the pulpit therefore any engagement in it must be authorized by him.

The pastor is responsible to insure the word that goes before the church is delivered from those who will feed and nurture it with sincerity and quality.

Invitations to preach are not granted based on right, friendship or "earned" privilege.

When themes are established for particular events or periods of time preachers are expected to adhere to them without excuse. Failure to do so will result in reduction of preaching opportunities.

All preachers are expected to be prepared to preach at any time. All are expected to live in perpetual preparation.

Preachers are expected to be in the pulpit on time and prepared for whatever the assignment may be.

The final authority on all prospective preachers must be approved by the pastor.

Only persons essential to the leadership and function of the worship are to sit in the pulpit. This reduces distraction to both the congregation and preacher.

Common entry into and out of the pulpit is not acceptable.

The pulpit is a station for the proclamation of the gospel therefore things such as announcement and non-ministry related proclamations are to be made from the floor and not the pulpit.

Entertainment has no place in the pulpit.

The pulpit is a place of respect and authority therefore no activity in it should reflect otherwise.

Ushers dress the pulpit with all things prior to the service and enhance it as needed during the course of the service.

# WHAT EVERY PASTOR OUGHT TO KNOW ABOUT BAPTISM

Baptism is one of the ordinances of the church.

Jesus was baptized prior to the commencement of His public ministry.

Baptism is commanded by Jesus to be done and in remembrance of Him.

Baptism does not save anyone.

Baptism is both real and symbolic.

Baptism is by immersion.

Church membership is not the goal of baptism and it should not be taught as an indoctrination ritual.

Only those who have made a profession of faith in the Lordship of Jesus should be baptized.

There is no mystical baptismal formula. Whether one is baptized in the name of the Father, Son and Holy Ghost or baptized in the name of Jesus.

Baptism symbolizes the presentation, death, burial and resurrection of our Lord Jesus Christ.

Baptism is to be conducted by the pastor or by ordained designees.

Baptism is not restricted to a particular time or place. It may be at the conclusion of a service or several weeks down the road.

# WHAT EVERY PASTOR OUGHT TO KNOW ABOUT BUSINESS MEETINGS

Business meetings are services of the church and should be conducted in an orderly and Godly manner.

Business meetings are for members only.

The pastor is the chairperson of the business meeting.

In the absence of the pastor from the business meeting he may appoint a designate at his discretion to fulfill his duties.

No business meeting is to be called without approval of the pastor.

The pastor may not schedule business meeting indiscriminately except in matters of emergency or extreme importance.

Business meetings should be established on a scheduled basis to permit the membership to make plans to be at them.

Business meetings should have a set time to start and to end.

Business meetings should have a set agenda and be governed by it. Issues that may arise during the course of one may be set aside for address at the next.

Business meetings should include written and oral reports that are turned in as an official part of the church records.

Business meetings shall not disclose personal giving records of any member for this is not legal nor proper.

All active members are entitled to copies of minutes, financial reports and reports at business meetings whether they are share in hard copy or electronic.

All records of the church are to remain on the church premises and in church files at all times. Copies may be made to edit and refine but official documentation is to remain.

All records are to be signed off on by the recording secretary, dated and sealed once approved by the church conference.

# WHAT EVERY PASTOR OUGHT TO KNOW ABOUT COMMUNION

Communion is an ordinance of the church.

Communion commemorates the life of Jesus in memorial fashion.

Communion and the Lord's Supper are the same thing.

The Bread in communion is representative of the body of Jesus given for us.

The Fruit of the Vine is representative of the shed blood of Jesus for our sins.

The Partakers of communion are only to be believers. It is not a common activity for everybody.

The time of taking it is not a set one. The rule is that as often as you do it you proclaim the Lord's death until He returns therefore it is at the discretion of the local assembly when and how often they do.

Communion is typically led by the pastor and ordained deacons, stewards or elders.

There is no sin in anyone else handling the elements for often it is the duty of deaconesses and other women to either bake the actual bread or to dress the communion table in its entirety.

The bread and fruit of the vine do not become the actual blood and body of our Lord. They are representative of them but not the realities.

One need not be a member of a particular local assembly to partake in communion. They need to be Christian but communion has its base not in denominational polity but in redemptive relationship.

# WHAT EVERY PASTOR OUGHT TO KNOW ABOUT BABY DEDICATIONS

Baby dedications are for the children of those who are saved and desire to dedicate their child to the Lord.

Baby dedications witness that the parents of a child are giving their child to the Lord to be raised in His word and ways.

Persons inclusive in dedications are (1) Parents (2) Grandparents and (3) God Parents. These persons are included on the record for the child.

Baby dedications are worship services and shall be integrated and conducted as such.

Baby dedications are not the same as christenings or infant baptisms and do not grant the baby church membership.

A child cannot be dedicated to the Lord whose parents have not dedicated themselves to the Lord.

Baby dedications are to be requested at least four weeks prior to the desired date and must be approved by the pastor.

A meeting with the pastor and/or pastoral staff will take place before the dedication to facilitate proper understanding of the service and how it is to take place.

A record of all dedications shall be maintained in the church files with a copy being given to parents.

# WHAT EVERY PASTOR OUGHT TO KNOW ABOUT WEDDINGS

All weddings are worship services.

All weddings held at the church are Christian in nature and officiated by ordained clergy.

Non-Christian ceremonies shall be held at the church.

Pastoral discretion is maintained in who the pastor marries.

All fees that may be incurred for ceremonies in accordance with church bylaws shall be paid 3 weeks prior to the ceremony to insure proper arrangements and staff are available and scheduled to take care of the need.

All services are to be planned with the pastor and are to be approved by the pastor before being planned.

The wedding service is overseen by the pastor with wedding planner being representative of the couple. Decisions and adjustments in ceremony that must be made are done at the pastor's discretion in collaboration with wedding planner.

In the event that another minister is requested to perform any ceremony there must be a request made to the pastor through the church and approval given following the meeting of pastor with said individual.

All rehearsals are to be scheduled in accordance with church calendar and are to last no longer than two hours.
All music requested during services is to be in good taste and in keeping with Christian tradition as are all other elements of the service.

Management of the sanctuary shall be under the direction of a church representative and in working with custodial staff. Adjustments to heat, air and moving of any furniture or equipment shall be stone by staff and not the wedding party.

Florists, photographers, videographers and other technical people shall be required to submit a plan for what they desire to do and the logistics required to accomplish their assignment. Free reign is not permitted without such plans.

Pastoral counseling is required for any wedding that is to take place in the sanctuary whether it be with pastor of the church or one referred by the pastor.

All marriage licenses are to be submitted to the pastor prior to the wedding and signed. The delivery of the license to the clerk of courts is the responsibility of the bride and groom however a copy of the wedding license shall be maintained at the church office in event there is a need for validation of the marriage or any other need pertaining to it.

# WHAT EVERY PASTOR OUGHT TO KNOW ABOUT FUNERALS

You only get one time to either do a funeral right or do it wrong.

Never approach a family unprepared to deal with your own personal emotions first. You must gather yourself before you reach out to others.

The pastor shall meet with the family along with other necessary church/pastoral staff to console them and to assist in meeting their transitional needs, help with arrangements and provide guidance.

Pastor and church staff shall work with the funeral home after meeting with the family in the scheduling of all services and facilitating smooth transitions at the church.

No funerals shall be planned without pastoral involvement.

Final service shall be done in collaboration with the family and sensitive to their needs in all ways.

No funeral shall begin without pastoral approval.

No service is ever to negate the fact that we are there to celebrate or commemorate the life of the person who has passed.

Although there may be an evangelistic appeal made in the service it is not to become an evangelism rally and opportunity to preach around the needs of the family.

The eulogy suggests praise and therefore it ought to be inclusive of aspects of the person's life that are historical, real and praiseworthy.

The eulogy should not exhaust the family nor disturb them unnecessarily.

All fraternal and masonic rituals are requested to be done at the funeral home or the cemetery but not during the sanctuary service.

All funerals are worship services.

All funerals are to be understanding, worshipful and therapeutic in nature.

There should be no repeated saying of "Now to this bereaved family" … "You loved them but God loved them best" … "The deceased has already preached his/her funeral" and "I came to preach to the living not to the dead."

The funeral is an event of celebration and compassion.

The pastor is the officiant or may appoint an officiant of all funerals although a different eulogist may be used with pastoral approval.

The funeral is to be both timely yet without rushing the family through final time with loved one.

Pastoral follow-up shall occur one week and one month following the funeral to help family with grief management and life transitions.

# WHAT EVERY PASTOR OUGHT TO KNOW ABOUT HOSPITAL VISITATION

Know what operation or procedure has taken place of the person you are visiting.

Seek to contact and pray with the individual prior to operation or procedure.

Go with a specific purpose in mind not merely to be there.

Do not go to the hospital immediately following and operation to visit the patient.

Confer with other family members in charge of oversight to schedule most appropriate time to visit.

Avoid asking too many questions about the reason for the stay or other personal questions in an open setting.

Do not sit on the bed when visiting.

Restrict you visit to 15 minutes unless something arises that requires your presence longer.

Determine if your visit is for the family well-being or for the patient.

Before bringing flowers or other items please insure that they are permissible and beneficial to the patients well-being.

# WHAT EVERY PASTOR OUGHT TO KNOW ABOUT BUDGET AND PLANNING

Budgets and calendars are essential to strategic planning.

A calendar shows where your intentions are.

A budget tells where your investments will be.

For every calendar item you must attach a budget to it.

Calendars discipline time and space thereby keeping operations fluid.

Calendars allow you to incorporate more people in the overall church operations.

Budgets permit people to give to causes that they may not otherwise know were existent or available to give to.

Budgets permit you to have church approval prior to events without having to schedule meetings for everything you desire to do.

Budgets reduce conflicts over money spent and who spends it.

Calendars permit you to schedule your life around established events and encourages people to respect your time also.

When possible make certain that you include certain things in your family life that others need to know, respect and honor.

Calendars schedule time for professional development, conventions, ministry opportunities, vacations and other necessary times.

Calendars enable you to maintain control over your life. Be certain to have a manager of your calendar if you do not handle it well and let nothing be added to it without your approval.

# WHAT EVERY PASTOR OUGHT TO KNOW ABOUT DEALING WITH MISTAKES

Mistakes are a part of being human. Do not expect perfection and you can deal with matters.

You may recover from a mistake if you do not give it more power than it actually has.

Give others room to be imperfect so that they may be transparent in their relationship with you.

Pastors lead imperfect churches.

Pastors give imperfect answers sometimes.

Expect that others will make mistakes dealing with you and things that matter most.

Most mistakes are not meant to hurt you therefore be as patient with others as you desire them to be with you.

Many sincere people will make the same mistake more than once.

Mistakes require that you confess. correct. cleanse, change and challenge yourself never to do the same thing again.

Admit when you fail before others that they might know how to do the same before you.

Mistake literally means we take something we should not have.

The word perfecting implies that we try more than once to arrive at perfection with because we fail sometimes in the process/

Realize that sometimes everyone else will be right and you will be wrong.

You must preach words that help others recover from mistakes.

You must sometimes live out publicly mistakes that you thought would always be private.

God often comes us out of hiding to face both himself and ourselves that our mistake might not cause us to live in shame and fear for the rest of our lives.

Remember mistakes of others and yourself for only short times.

# WHAT EVERY PASTOR OUGHT TO KNOW ABOUT PLAGARIZING SERMONS

Do not get in the habit of echoing the sermons of others without authorization from God.

If you are going to preach the sermon of another, take the time to feel, understand and communicate it differently that the one you heard it from.

If the word that you preach is not one that you have labored in you are not worthy to preach it.

Every sermon you preach has been shared by others in other contexts before. Water that runs through one fountain runs from another also. Just make sure you are connected to the source and not stealing from another's well.

Do not let commentaries and other study tools make you lazy by preaching them and not the word. Process your understanding and release it afterwards.

Write your message on the page and understand that using the quotes and knowledge of others as seasoning in it.

There is no credit given to the one who recites and repeats a word that he/she has not received.

Do not use information that is above you. People know when you have received what you share and when you are sharing what you do not know.

Do not tolerate plagiarism from those who come from under your authority.

Giving credit to others in your preaching does not make you

a lesser preacher. It enriches you and connect you with other great minds and people.

If you use what others share extensively, build upon it and leave it richer than it was when you got it.

You cannot say "Thus Says the Lord" if you did not stand in his presence and hear Him say it.

It is possible to preach a good word that you were never authorized to say and be totally out the will of God.

Because you preached it does not believe that it all belongs to you. Similarity in sharing does not mean others are stealing from you.

# WHAT EVERY PASTOR OUGHT TO KNOW ABOUT CLOSINGS AND INVITATIONS

There cannot be great closings in preaching if there has been no great opening or disclosure in preaching.

Whooping is a mechanic in preaching not an empowerment of the Spirit. It is used by the Spirit but it is not nor should it ever be used as a substitute for the Spirit.

Do not despise the whoop or the squall that may be employed in the expression of others. Hear and enter the celebration rather than miss it because of how it was done.

Celebration at the end of a sermon may be done in different manners. Pick where and how you will celebrate but make sure that it does not drown the message.

Preaching comes to an end and ought to always leave people with a decision to make.

Planning the close of a message is a good exercise for it gives you an exit strategy rather than leaving you wandering in a message already finished.

If the message was gentle, please do not slam it closed when you finish.

Going by Calvary in a message does not mean that it is always part of the end of the message. It is always part of the service but do not try to attach it to every closing of the message you preach.

Closing fit the flow of the message. Do not force what is not there.

Call and response is a communication between the pew and the pulpit that often generates a rhythm of worship that you cannot create on your own.

Excitement without edification is emotion in error.

Invitations are first to Christ and not church.

Invitations offer the Kingdom Citizenship before church membership.

Be careful that what you are inviting people to receive is available.

Invitations should always focus on the Lordship of Christ and not the governance of the local congregation.

# WHAT EVERY PASTOR OUGHT TO KNOW ABOUT PEOPLE WHO DISAGREE WITH YOU

Because a person disagrees with you does not mean they are against you.

People who disagree with you are not necessarily your enemies.

Disagreement does not mean that one does not love or support you.

Never let disagreement become the mother of a grudge.

Sometimes you must pay closer attention to your greatest critics than your greatest supporters because they will make you aware of things your closest friends cannot see due to the clouds of admiration they see you behind.

Do not shun disagreement but seek to understand such people.

Do not ignore disagreement but work through it to a consensus.

If you cannot come to agreement with others and they cannot do so with you, take the results and trash them. Work towards agreement together.

Learn to disagree with others without becoming disagreeable in your relationship

Do not favor the agreeable more than the disagreeing.

Disagreement and argument are two different things. Disagreement has an outlet. Arguments often have no outlet.

Have fair fights and when you walk away be able to have a better not lesser relationship.

Leave a disagreement as a disagreement. It is no more than that.

There does not have to be a right or wrong in some cases. There is just a difference of opinion.

# WHAT EVERY PASTOR OUGHT TO KNOW ABOUT ARMOR BEARERS

Armor Bearers are not a biblical office for preachers and should not be taught as such.

Armor Bearers must never be those who simply carry things for you and make your work easier.

Armor Bearers ought to be well qualified and disciplined warriors in the faith competent to companion and cover you in times of battle.

Armor Bearers out to be honored and not treated as less than the best of support persons.

Armor Bearers need not be people of deficient or absent mind. Their loyalty does not mean they do not have the right to disagree.

Armor Bearers must be able to be trusted with your weaknesses and vulnerabilities therefore do no select or keep one that you do not trust.

Armor Bearers need to be privy to what is going on in your movements in ministry so that they may know how to best provide support for you.

Armor Bearers are not security details. Do not use them as bodyguards if that is not what they are.

Never ask your armor bearer to do demeaning things.

# A SHEPHERD'S HEART

# 'A PLEA FOR REVIVAL

Revival will not begin with more preaching events and conferences held only among those who already know or have a hint at the truth. Revival will begin in the hearts and souls of those who know God and submit themselves in prayer for an enacting of His will and work in their personal lives.

It will not increase with gifted preachers increasing in popularity and traveling the country preaching to crowds only to have the fizz like Coke poured fast then fade in fullness with time. It will not begin with momentarily moved persons coming down the aisle to say the "sinner's prayer" without truly receiving the Jesus as Lord. It will not begin with people coming to the altar to enter the Kingdom and returning with membership certificates but no crosses. It will not begin with an event but a true experience.

We are truly living in the last moments of the last days and the time has come to seek God truthfully. Churches cannot continue to do the convenient things and believe that in the right time they can call on God to intervene in our affairs. Our focus and agendas must change. Our theology must become real and our declarations to others must be with integrity and openness. This is not an easy road. This is not a simple decision. This is not fire insurance. This is not a boring and restrictive religion of rules. This is not an isolated journey of just me and God. THE church DOES have people very much like the people that you have learned to get along with in other areas of your life.

We're not perfect people and sometimes we are not even good. Yes, God has a standard. No, everything is not acceptable. Despite contemporary intellectual thought and scientific assessments along with psychology and philosophical development WE BELIEVE that Satan is real, Hell is a place and judgment will occur despite the feel that it is fantasy and far too harsh. Jesus is the only way to God and no man is better than another man based on any criteria we may set in this life.

The preacher must stand in the presence of God and upon the wall of community declaring the vision with voice that is clear and commanding. We must cease running around the wall bellowing what is not pertinent or real to the people. If you fear heights, you cannot stand upon it. We must become present and exemplary not by having no fault but by living out the gospel among the people not as being distanced. Our revival meetings have become multitudinous but our people starve.

Our country walks further from God. Now is the time for return. Now is the time where the heart of people must return to the Spirit of God. The time has come for the people of God to restore God in their hearts and take His work in our hands. The silent witness and clandestine commitments are no longer acceptable. The move of God shall not begin in the sanctuary but in the soul. Yielding and transformation shall provide the kindling that can save our people and restore communities. This is not a preacher thing and the responsibility for it cannot be paid by contributing to someone else to do it in your stead. Stand up and be recognized. HE IS LORD! Now is the time. Let your heart be broken, your eyes saturated, your mind renewed, your hands lifted and your voice heard. '.

# REFOCUSING ON THE POWER OF GOD

Many services have become compelling to the masses because they are promoted as being those in which you can expect a mighty move of God. The expectation often is that after the preacher has delivered THE WORD of God that the individual will receive a word from God or that there will be healings and what we typically call "Slaying in the Spirit" where people go out under the power of God.

I do not belittle nor underestimate when God moves in this manner. I believe that many services when the presence of God authentically moves in this manner are truly wonderful and necessary. However, to many are equating these as the defining manner in which we experience the power of God.

The power of God is not a periodic surge that is operative only at particular times and administered by a particular surge creator. It is a continuing current that is to flow in the spirit and life of the believer that is the generative force in his or her life. It is 'dunamis" or the dynamite of God operative in daily demonstration in our interaction with others.

The reason that many miss the true power in them is that they are more fascinated with lamps and bulbs than they are with power. The beauty of a lamp in in its design, color and shade. The combination can be stunning to look at and when you include uniquely designed bulbs with brilliance that takes over the darkest room of that can be toned down to create the sexiest atmosphere many are impressed. They celebrate the lamp and are carried away by it not recognizing that what makes the lamp shine is the power operative in it.

We must be careful not to give too much credit to our bulbs, shades and colors. We must not fail to realize that the power of God is in us. The indwelling of the Holy Spirit enables you to become and operate in the authority and character of God. You have access on a daily basis just as the lamp has power as long as it is plugged into the source. Many light sources operate on two source and are referred to as AC/DC. Battery operated power and electrical power are the sources. Batteries run down but may appear to be as brilliant as electricity for a moment. However, they are temporal. When they burn out they are replaced and we move on. The electricity lives in current. It flows and is present as long as the river flows.

Cease operating on the temporal sources. You have access to the unceasing flow of God. Connect yourself and experience the power of God not only on the floor but as you walk upright. You can be healed on the other side of the benediction and the prophet can declare to you as you walk by the way as well as in a private word in the sanctuary. God speaks in the message of the preached word and sometimes that is the only word you need to hear. Operate in the power that is in you. Plug in and turn the battery off. Let it flow.

# A PRAYER FOR MY NATION

Heavenly Father, I come on behalf of my beloved nation to ask your blessings upon us. I pray a prayer of restoration for we are indeed a great people and I am so proud to be an American. I am proud of my heritage and what it represents overall. I stand as a privileged individual and committed to her defense and dignity. I love it and I thank you for what you have created me in her.

I come as one among many with responsibilities that need to be owned that have been neglected for years. I stand in repentance for although we invoke your name in many ways we do not honor you as we speak of. We have gone away from what you have spoken and your word has become one among many words that we have adhered too.

The authority of who you are is obscured and though we do not call it such we have become as the Greeks who met Paul on Mars Hill with altars built to many gods. Your presence in our morality is intrusive and offensive. Your presence in our schools is tolerated but only silently lest you should disturb the learning processes of others who do not honor you. Your presence in our halls of justice is challenged and even in our churches too often we have intellectualized, socialized, politicized, race based, denomination divided and economically isolated and polarized ourselves in so many ways that we appear as parts existing rather than a healthy whole body.

Guns blaze in the streets and cities burn in riots and responses to injustice that are obviously tolerated. Communities suffer, children rule the homes and schools have become too often habitations and dens for the perpetuation of a continuing educational decline. Toys are more focused on than tools and a generation is so buried in play that the prospects of it increasing in growth diminish with each new Nintendo Version or I-Phone.

Father I cringe that we have no time for authentic revival in a desert place. Our time is consumed and prayer is not necessary to make it work. Our services are much shorter and our influence is steadily diminishing. We are struggling with you even remaining the one over "our church." Preaching is taking a weak turn and the voice too often speaking has not recently heard.

The pastoral influence in many areas has diminished and shepherds are held hostage lest their share of the wool be withheld and another be appointed over the flock by others. The position of popularity has overtaken the one of power and the adjustments to appease the "itching ear crowd" has rendered a distortion in the heavenly realm and many sermons returned because the Holy Spirit could not sign off on what was not yours.

Faith is no longer the key to transformation and even your perpetual presence in the daily affairs of the nation is up for vote while we determine where we will place you even if you win election. I sound like a foolish man but this is the truth of what is happening in our nation. The beauty of diversity has become burdensome and we have victimized too many on the basis of skin color rather than genuine identity. We have sinned Lord.

We have gone away from you yet call you only too often only when we need a religious validation for something we want to do that appeases a segment of your people. We are the wealthiest nation overall upon the planet yet the needs of those beneath the top 5% are drastically unmet and too many of our people go hungry and live beneath the poverty line. Forgive us for how we have judged others while violating our own people and your standards of justice, peace and love. You said, "If my people which are called by my name would humble themselves and pray and seek my face that you would hear from heaven, forgive our sins and heal our land.

# GOD IS GOING TO GIVE YOU A SHIFT
## "Understanding and Implications"

A phrase commonly heard today is that "God is going to give a shift." It is often repeated and is very true. It is powerful and prophetic. It is a call to preparation and a reconstruction. Its popularity should not cause us to miss its deeper meaning.

Let the statement be heard and interpreted in the right manner. God is going to "Shift." This word shift is different than the word "sway." As I talk to some I hear more of the sense that He is going to just move things. The opinion seems to be that the shift is going to be as God moving strongly in the branches of a tree and stirring it. I believe that this does happen in the environment of the Kingdom but when we speak of "a shift" this is not what we are speaking of.

A shift is a disruptive thing. It goes beneath the obvious and engages foundations. It renders the current foundation inadequate in its current position and strength for what is coming. It fortifies, enriches and expands the sphere of influence and engagement in the hidden places and provides for a move in the obvious that cannot occur without it.

While occurring there are things that happen in the life of a being or building that are disturbing. Comfort levels are disrupted. Cracks in walls may become apparent. Hunger for more is realized. Things are torn out that have always been a part of your life and your capacity to handle more grows. This is not comfortable and the shifting in you affects every relationship and identity you have. You must be willing to yield to the Master's reconstructive plan and at times admit that you do not understand the full plan.

Sometimes life renders us useful but antiquated. We have not upgraded the deeper self in a long time. The church of this day must move with God and not AS God. We cannot be the determiners of our destiny and what we were a few decades ago or even a few years ago will not be sufficient for what God would have us to be in the next few years.

There is a new call and shift to a true sense of holiness and accountability. So often when that word is used the mind runs to "self-righteousness" rather than the true essence of the word. Jesus said, "Upon this rock I will build MY church...Matthew 16" That means that it is holy unto Him. It is His and subject to His Kingdom principles and directives. The expansion that is coming is coming to those who will yield themselves to Him. The foundations must be strengthened and expanded for there are churches, ministries, communities and kingdom enterprises that must rise and become more visible and receptive as well as those who will broaden their current levels.

Churches built on mere membership shall fold to those constructed on developing disciples. The lifestyle shall feed communities and the church shall have an agenda that is not constricted to Wednesday/Sunday. It will move into the real community and embrace people where they are. It will shift from a one horse wagon to a multi-saint powered engine build and certified by the Holy Spirit. The preaching, praise and worship shall shift to a perpetually engaging ministry that can be effective no matter the circumstances or day. The congregational chemistry shall shift for the local community shall bow before God and tilt the stance of many churches that maintain the hard line and refuse to allow God to move in them. Such churches that maintain that line shall ultimately be condemned not because they were bad but because they refused to shift and are no longer adequate for divine usage.

This shift is a move of God. Several years ago many Catholic churches closed in the United States. The presence of Catholic Schools and Ministries in these neighborhoods had diminished and the burden of tragic priestly scandals cast a dim view upon much work and a distrust among the guilty as well as the guiltless. People who were catholic at school were Baptist, Methodist and Pentecostal in faith expression particularly in African American Communities.

There was no shift that the Catholic Church made to deal with changing population and cultural faith tradition.

Beautiful Edifices were sold at incredibly low prices and many other churches jumped at the thought of being able to acquire these facilities. Gorgeous were these facilities but many of the new owners failed to realize the price of high ceilings and boiler/steam operated heating systems. If the facilities were to operate efficiently and cost effectively there would need to be shifts in ceilings and shifts in electrical construction. HVAC systems, insulation, wiring, wall reconstruction, painting and more would need to occur. They would need to shift from what the building and ministry had been to what it needed to become. Many returned the buildings or let them foreclose. Why? Because they did not want to pay the cost of the shift.

The illustration speaks to the current state of the church. It is a time for another shift. God is moving in the hidden places. When the shift comes please be ready. It may be a little disruptive but it is so very necessary that our cause in the Kingdom might be recognized and our place rendered worthy of where we stand.

# THE DIMINISHING PRESENCE OF GOD

The atmosphere is filled with religion. Churches fill communities throughout the nation. Signs share the meeting times. Clergy abound in abundance. Choirs are in rehearsal and ministries keep providing a variety of very helpful and needed services.

Industry has become filled with Christians particularly music, books and movies. Some of the world's most prosperous entrepreneurs are Christians and there is nothing wrong with that. Intrigue has gripped many who do not really desire to know God but want to follow a few of His people around and "capitalize" on their "realities."

The word is preached by many capable persons. Conferences and meetings are held in abundance and streamed globally all over the world. Multi-Media has made the sharing of the Gospel much more effective. Apostles, bishops, and pastors have flooded new venues and assumed new pulpits and parishes. Fees have become more associated with preaching and ministering than offering. The Great Commission has become a repeated but dysfunctional reality in the hearts and minds of many. Yet the declaration that the Gospel must be preached globally remains a great part of the modern Christian front.

It speaks these words to commend us for many jobs well done. I commend us for great ministries and teachings. I commend us for great music and entertainment. I commend us for great books written and conference meetings that excite and elevate us BUT in this dark and dismal day in which we live I raise the question WHERE IS THE VOICE OF GOD?

The question seems answered in the activities but that is not so. Deeds are excellent Christian service but they are not the VOICE of God. Much that is enacted in the name of the church is good but it is not the primary mandate of the Lord. Sometimes the promotion of the church and its work overshadows the work of God and His Kingdom. Often the presentation of the personality of those who are out front takes precedence over the God whom they represent. The sweet oratory or music that emerges from our voices must never become the substitute for the voice of God in our lives.

As we continue many people no longer look for a word from God but seek a word about their circumstance that will make life a little better. The entrance into the true presence of God has few ushers and the sanctuary is not the place that is a place for meeting God. I cringe that often when God speaks many cannot hear for they have not been told that you must be born again to have an ear to hear what the Spirit says to the Church.

Do not get me wrong, many can hear about God but when God exposes Himself to us at the deepest level you must give yourself to Him to experience it. In this era too much of what we offer in our churches is a buffet of spiritual salads, bread, deserts and drinks minus the authentic entree' THE VOICE OF GOD.

Who speaks for God? NOT about Him but HIM. Who has stood in the counsel of God and allowed Him to fill him or her and then released the authentic word given? The power of preaching is in its authentic origin and operation. Can God sign off on the word I last preached? In eternity shall He claim it as His or shall it burn as kindling in the incinerator of fruitlessness?

It is not my intellect, my character, my charm or humor that is the focal point here although God can certainly use them. There is no power in the mechanics of a whoop, a holler, a squall or any other celebratory expression that has power but it is in what and who is celebrated.

When the VOICE OF GOD is heard sometimes we should just be still. We may sit in paralyzed participation. We tremble at the thought that He engages us as He does. He inspires the sense of awe that does not call us to clap but to bow. It calls us to repent and rise to a deeper sense of love, honor and duty. When the voice of God is heard the preacher's tone is not the focal point and the voice of the evil one is silence.

When the voice of God is heard the sheep come forward and wolves tremble for fear of disclosure. When the voice of God is heard the benediction establishes a commencement that embraces the next week and mandates that certain things declared in heaven already be manifested on earth. When the Voice of God is Heard...

However

As we progress it diminished more and more. Although He speaks to us still it becomes more faint. We have live in the canyons of Christian experience and sought to thrive off the echoes of voices that have spoken here previously. The time is now for that Voice to be released again in us and through us. SILENCE is mandated in some areas lest the noise of the event become mistaken for the true voice of God. As we listen we shall hear more. As we hear more and heed it He shall speak. Indeed, the diminishing voice shall give volume again to a world in need of it. AMEN

# SITTING IN HIS PRESENCE

Environments affect us in many ways. I believe that the sun invites me to take it in and celebrate its power and stimulation. It welcomes me to new days and impacts my perspective on the day. When I do not see it I find myself sluggish and without the vibrancy that I have when it is there. I love to bask in its presence.

Rainy and snowy days are cuddling days. The environment they create makes me want to stay in and take it easy. Although I love going out in them for certain activities for the most part they draw me to intimate times.

Ballparks get me excited. I do not go to them to sit somberly but to cheer and get riled up. I go to cheer for my team and challenge the other team. I go to participate in the activities of the crowd and if there are none I create some. I love the environment.

I go to church because I enjoy the corporate worship environment. I love being in the presence of God with my brothers and sisters. I am taught and exhorted. I am reproved and at times rebuked. I sing, I pray, I preach, I love it. The environment blesses me.

There are many more environment I enjoy but one that I feel that we all need to take more time to enjoy is just Sitting in the Presence of God. Yes! That sounds simple but it is so necessary. As I mentioned earlier, I love a sunny environment. I love the warmth that I receive and the beauty that the sun creates in the numerous places that I encounter it.

I need no company to enjoy it. I need no sound. I need no special time or place. I just step into it and allow it to affect me as it will. I do that with the rain and the snow also. The longer I stay the deeper the effect on my total being. I respond to it because I allow it to affect me. I prepare for it by not wearing a fur coat on a sunny summer day and not wearing shorts on a blistering winter day.

Why not enter the presence of God solely with the purpose of being there? Sometimes the deepest form of worship is not when your words flow and the surroundings you are in are perfect. Sometimes simply to sit before God with no sound or actions allows Him to bathe you in His essence and spray you with His fragrance. He can warm you and comfort you simply by overshadowing you. He can refresh you and cause you to rest because of the winds that He blows upon your soul and the tender raindrops of compassion that He permits to fall upon the canopy of your mind while making you to lie down. He welcomes you and desires you to simply come and linger with Him for a while.

Many feel that there is no worship unless there is activity and words flowing. Many mask a causal relationship with God in a crowd of others in the same condition who speak of Him to whom the seldom speak to. True love for God like tea needs time to steep without being stirred. There is a true blessing in dwelling in his presence alone.

No requests, no pains, no problems, no praise reports and no other verbal communication. Sometimes we must go into His presence for the pleasure and purpose of being with God. "Come unto me..." is an invitation to dwell where He is that He might be and do for you as He pleases. You are his regular attendee and because you dare spend this type of time with God you become open to intimacy with Him and communication on a level not accessible to the mere Midweek/Sunday person.

I wonder what a service would be like if a whole congregation sat silently in the presence of God for 2 hours and let Him affect them all. I wonder if God would recognize them and if He could be worshiped by the attendees. Could we walk away as the pale person who bathes in the sun for the same period with an obvious effect upon us because of the environment that lingers past the moment that we are present? I just wonder... It is indeed possible.

Come to the place of true relationship and power. Come to the secret place and be silent as He affects you with His presence, His power and His purpose. No agenda needed. Cast of all concerns and be still while you sit in His presence. The affect is guaranteed. He has a space for you that is waiting. You may enter it now

# THE WORD WE PREACH
## Incarnate Involvement

John 1:14 ~"and the Word became flesh and dwelt among us and we beheld His glory" Jesus was not a hidden savior. He is not God lurking in the shadows trying to do something undercover. Jesus was not God trembling before men and seeking to get in and out of a service. He is a visible and vibrant savior. When He came He sought to be close to us. He sought to identify with us in our situations and selves. "The Word became flesh..." He was interested in identifying with us in our same situations.

In the book of Isaiah, the prophet declares that in the year King Uzziah died he saw the Lord high and lifted up and the train of His robe filled the temple. What a depiction! The picture is awesome. The Lord stood in eternal majesty with glory exuding from him and angelic chorus blaring the original rendition of Holy, Holy, Holy. This one who stood there and whose voice shook the doorposts of the temple comes to us in garment radically different that we might identify with Him. He comes into our neighborhood because we could not come into His...YET. He did not run through it but He dwelt, He lingered, He stayed, He moved in, He pitched His tent...He did not run away or hide out. He did not run through on Sunday and not be seen throughout the week. He showed us that you cannot save what you are not there to reach out to.

The coming of Jesus teaches us that it is our task to become what is necessary to enable others to become what God desires. For Jesus to become one like us He had to step down from where he was. he has to move in and live the life under the circumstances that He desires for us to live. He does not give instructions from afar but in the midst of what has hurt and destroyed us. Jesus teaches that true ministry requires that we move in and build relationships that have lasting impact. You cannot change a world or make it better if you bark instructions untried from a remote place to others. You and I must pay the cost of identification.

The contemporary church struggles in this area. We are situated in areas that often we are not incarnate in. We meet in them but we do not move in. We do not have an effective strategy for identification and involvement. We have a house but have not made ourselves at home in it. "The Word dwelt among us..." He did so from the beginning and was there until He died. He sends us to communities to DWELL among them... Jerusalem, Judea, Samaria, utmost parts of the world. We are to dwell among them in a visible manner.

Let us live the season and intent of our Savior. Let us get involved tangibly and visibly with our community. Let us learn and share in the situations of our fellow man and exemplify the life and purpose that HE desires. You cannot build a better world or community if you are not willing to get to work in it. Instruction is good but the real work is never done without involvement.

# INSIGHTS

Do you still think you can make an impact?" I said "yes, but why all these searching questions? I am still on the team. That person said "Good! But you are not properly on the field or in the game. Get back to doing what you do that too few folks know you do." I looked perplexed and convicted. That person looked certain about their words and winked while walking away. I snarled "know it all" but I got the message.

The ultimate goal in preaching is not to hear the congregation say AMEN but to hear the Father say WELL DONE
.
Preaching meetings are not revival
.
A revival is not a time of preaching without purpose or passion before a congregation without preparation and hunger for a deeper relationship with God. It is opening oneself wide to a fresh spiritual encounter and engagement with the Spirit of God with an intent of being renewed and refreshed in every way

Contemporary ministers must return to preaching The Word of God. Motivation and other speeches are necessary and have their rightful place but there is an authority in the Word of God that is revelatory and authoritative. We are at our best when we can say more than this and this and say This says the Lord.

In my reflections on life I realize that I have been in ministry for 35 years. I have been preaching for almost 34 and I have so much left to learn. The closer I get to God the more I see my own imperfections as do others. Sometimes others think that I have it all together because I am a preacher but I hurriedly remind them that I am a preacher by calling and commitment but still a creature. I have issues like everyone else so do not put me too high in your estimation. Honor the God in me. You will too find that no matter how good you seek to live you have flaws and issues but that is okay. Keep flying closer to the flame. God does not expect you to be perfect. He looks to perfect you.

A friend of mine told me that I should never preach what I have not perfected in living. He continued that it is hypocritical to share with others how to live when you have problems yourself. I told him that that the Word always speaks from above and gives direction to situations beneath. If you wait to be perfect before you share HE who is perfect, you will die without HIM perfecting you.

If I could preach one message to the world for one occasion it would be "The Complete Love of God" He loves us exceptionally; He loves us inclusively; He loves us individually; He loves us eternally... He loves us beyond the US that we know... THAT IS LOVE!

Contemporary ministers must return to preaching The Word of God. Motivation and other speeches are necessary and have their rightful place but there is an authority in the Word of God that is revelatory and authoritative. We are at our best when we can say more than this and this and say This says the Lord.

# EARSHOTS OF EXPERIENCE

Sometimes the best things in life come through unintended and unexpected sharing. The truth is an unplanned humorous encounter or a sudden announcement or truth that seems to be divinely placed and you walk away changed.

# WOULD YOU DO IT AGAIN?

Friend:
Rev. Would you pastor again

Me:
Yes, why do you ask?

Friend:
Because you have a lot of life left and I do not want you to
waste it.

Me:
So are you saying that if I am not pastoring I am wasting?

Friend:
No, but I needed to shock you and get you thinking. Get back on the
field.

Me:
As a pastor?

Friend:
Maybe...Maybe not! Just get back on the field and take your position
(hung up phone)

Me:
He thinks he told me! He really did!

(Maybe he told you too!)

# RELATIONSHIP EXPERT?

Man:
What makes you an expert on relationships?

Me:
I am a consultant not an expert. I work from a pastoral perspective.

Man:
Explain

Me:
I help people deal with issues within themselves and with others. I teach more principles and deal with more groups.

Man:
Like a psychiatrist, LPC or Psychologist?

Me:
No... they are much more clinical. I help people understand how to engage in healthy self-communication and practical relationships utilizing a biblical base.

Man:
You will have me talking to myself? I do not need your services. You will have me messed up with everyone else. You need a degree so people can talk with you and not themselves. Relationship Consultant? Yeah right! What do you have to say for yourself?

Me:
Consult with yourself and find an answer.

# DEAL

Member:
I have a problem with you

Me:
Oh!  What is it?

Member:
I feel the church pays you too much to preach on Sunday.

Me:
I see.  You may have a point.

Member:
You need to take a pay cut since you recognize this.

Me:
I will on the following conditions:  I get paid an hourly wage for all pastoral duties over 40 hours and since you want me to maintain office hours that time will go quickly.  I will need time and a half for evening hours. I will also require special payments for all weddings, funerals, dedications, visitations, counseling, emergency calls, jail runs, court settings and other things like that.

Member:
If you are not going to do it then who are we going to get to do it.

Me:
You must pay someone to do it.

# IS THAT SO?

Professor:
Pastor I have been teaching speech communication for the past 25 years and I want to tell you that people on the average only have an attention span of 20 minutes so anything you say after that they do not retain.

Pastor:
So what are you trying to say?

Professor:
I am saying that you must cut your sermons down so that we may get out earlier than we do. These 45 minute sermons are a bit taxing on the mind and the seat.

Pastor:
Professor how long are your classes?

Professor:
What does that have to do with anything?

Pastor:
Well, if the average high school class lasts 50 minutes and you say the attention span of the average person is only 20 minutes surely you do not hold the students accountable.

Professor:
I hold them to the highest standard of learning. I cut no corners and do not grade on a curve. If I teach it in the time I expect them to learn it

Pastor:
You are on your way to being one of the biggest hypocrites.

Professor: Why do you say that?

Pastor:
You hold them accountable for a less than exciting professor whose lectures are informative but not the stuff that keeps eyes open and you say you cannot bear with a message from a young, dynamo like me for less than you spend up there. I do not give tests and yet you complain.

Professor:
Teaching is different…

Pastor:
Okay then…come Sunday seeking to learn and remain after service so that I can give you the associated quiz. By the way, the message will be a full 50 minutes now. Just like your lecture.

Professor:
(Walking away defeated) I cannot stand him.

# APPENDIXES

# APENDIX I
# CHURCH LEADER AGREEMENT

I pledge to assume the role of leader with the understanding that I set the pace and provide the example for those that follow and learn from me.

I pledge that I shall be diligent in the fulfillment of my duties and in the development of it.

I pledge to be on time and to always be ready for what my task may be.

I pledge to grow as a leader and challenge others to grow through reading, practice and innovative engagements.

I pledge to be honest in my dealings and courteous in how I handle others.

I pledge to be faithful in my giving of treasure, talent and time.

I pledge to be supportive of my pastor and a communicator of directives that he may desire me to give even when such directives are not the ones I would give if in charge.

I pledge to speak well of my church and respectfully of other leaders.

I pledge not to bad mouth any member of this leadership team and to work in such a manner that when time comes for me to relinquish this position that a successor will not be difficult to find.

I pledge that at any time that I see that I cannot faithfully function in this position, I will step out of it without anger or having to be told to do so.

I pledge to lead in such a manner that when I place my service before the Lord He shall be able to say "Good and faithful servant, well done!

# APPENDIX II
## CHARGE TO CHURCH: PASTOR INSTALLATION

The person who stands before you is your pastor and your leader. This is the choice of the congregation and a leader who God has prepared to lead you in vision and in the growth of your church.

Your pastor cannot lead without your support and cannot make the church what it can be by himself. He is here because you have said that he is the Lord's choice for you therefore treat him as such by receiving this charge to do the following:

I charge you to stand with your Pastor. Let it be known at all times that he is not alone and that you are committed to the oneness of the body of Christ and the oneness of your church family.

I charge you to step with your Pastor. The movement of the church as one body is essential to its testimony in the world and its function within itself. Even when you are not in agreement it is important that someone be accountable for the direction of the church. You calling of this person today confirms your trust in his leadership as your head and your pledge to not only stand with but also to step with your pastor.

I charge you to serve your Pastor. The pastor is called to serve the congregation and in like manner the church should serve him. The church is charged to provide for the well-being of the pastor and family in a qualitative and sincere manner. The needs of his family are important including physical, spiritual, financial, social, emotional and mental. Muzzle not the ox that treads out the corn.

I charge you to support your Pastor. Provide and environment that facilitates his growth in every manner. Create a support staff that enables him to be more effective. Provide for their well-being that they may assist him in the provision of yours. Your growth increases his and his increases everyone's potentially.

I charge you to sit with your pastor. Take time to talk before you have to "really talk." Be confident and comfortable with conversing and knowing your pastor as a person and not an icon. Embrace the reality of the person without becoming obsessed in any manner with the office. Informal times of gathering are healthy for all members and permit your pastor to see another side of you also. Express yourself heart to heart and ask to meet with him as a church family just to share sometimes.

I charge you to share your pastor. Growth is inevitable and others shall become part of this congregation that will reduce the individual time that he may have with some. As Moses was required to have help in certain matters so shall it be that your pastor will not always be the one attending directly to your needs in every matter. Let the extensions of him help you without your feeling slighted or angry. Community and other organizations in it shall reach out to him and when they do, understand that they are reaching out to you also. Share him and yourselves with him.

I charge you to understand the humanity of your pastor. There will be times when he is tired, frustrated, angry, depressed, sad and wrong. There will be times when he has no answer or time to deal with what might seem pressing to you. He is a person of strength and with frailties that may not be yours. You will need to walk with him when you do not understand him, forgive him when he is not right, lift him when he is down and let him be down to earth and real.

I charge you to believe God for the vision and strive to do good together. Move beyond the view and give voice to what God speaks to you. What works for your congregation may not do so for the other so trust the vision of your pastor.

I charge you to be aware of serpents and of barking sheep who howl at the moon. I charge you not to take them into your fellowship and help your pastor in dealing with them in presence, doctrine and influence. Regardless of how popular or financial they are I charge you to recognize that sweet venom is still poisonous and fatal and a light bite can kill as quickly as a large one.

I charge you to keep the business of the church at the church. Be agreeable and not contentious. Be submissive and yet recognize your strong, necessary place.

I charge you to be a workman for the Kingdom. Your pastor is an equipper of equippers. He is a master craftsman in need of other toolmakers to help him supply what is needed to build a great church under the directive of the Holy Spirit. Use all that you have and create to the glory of God.

I charge you to serve this present age with the servant that you install this day so that the host of heaven and the militia on earth will know that you are faithful, forceful and forever serving together in an exemplary manner to the glory of the most high God.

I CHARGE YOU!

I charge you to love the people of God with the love that He gives to you to share with them.

I charge you to be exemplary in your conversation, in your conduct and in your considerations that the presence of God might be seen in you.

I charge you to love God in an obvious manner and teach others to do the same.

I charge you to be patient, forgiving, supportive, joyful, peaceful and meek in handling the people of God.

I charge you to recognize that this congregation is God's Church and not your crowd therefore let that be the governing consciousness you have in dealing with them.

I charge you to link the aged and the young that strength might run with wisdom and vision might fellowship with dreams.

I charge you to be strong enough to tell the truth yet wise enough to administer it in such a way that it will develop and not destroy.

I charge you to not forget that your first duty is to feed the church of God therefore give yourself to prayer, study, worship and meditation. Let not your life become so occupied that these become options and not obligations.

I charge you to be an example unto the men and walk as one of them never forgetting that when our savior entered this world He did so as a man.

I charge you to be an example unto our women that they might see in you what is good and desirable in a man of God and not fall into the snare of less than honorable men. I charge you to demonstrate how to relate to and reverence them to the benefit of their lives and the glory of God.

I charge you to preach to the people of God and not at them. I charge you to pray for them in all situations and at all times. I charge you to prepare them for the work of the Kingdom and its prosperity.

I charge you to protect them from pulpit predators, perverse prophets, corrupting congregants and delicious but deceiving doctrine.

I charge you to feed them, lead them weed them and seed them.

I charge you to care for this flock as Jesus would that they might arrive under your leadership to a place God has ordained to His glory.

I charge you!

# APPENDIX IV
## CHARGE TO MINISTER: LICENSING

I charge you to dedicate yourself to the study of the word.

I charge you to learn as much as you can that you might be sufficiently supplied in the time to share with others.

I charge you never to waste an opportunity to preach by coming to the pulpit unprepared.

I charge you to preach what you have studied and heard and not become a plagiarist or dispenser of half-truths, rumors and lies.

I charge you to dedicate yourself not only to the preaching of the word but the teaching of it also.

I charge you to live humbly before your pastor and learn what you have been called to in this manner.

I charge you to engage in daily study and meditation.

I charge you to learn from your pastor by example and to inquire of the ministry you engage in to learn even more.

I charge you to be ever growing and dedicated to the expansion of who you are and what you do.

I charge you to support others in ministry and never to expose in public faults or flaws you find in another.

I charge you to teach and learn not only the scriptures but how to administer them in all situations.

I charge you to be confidential in your dealings and faithful in your assignments.

I charge you to seek the progression and prosperity in understanding of the people every time you speak.

I charge you to devote yourself to the best until it becomes better and the better until it becomes best that your work might please God and enable you to continue to serve h
Him in more excellent ways.

I CHARGE YOU!

# APPENDIX V
# CHARGE TO CHURCH:
# MINISTER ORDINATION

I charge you to love and honor one who stands before you to the glory of God.

I charge you to be supportive in every way.

I charge you to encourage the growth and provide the environment and tools to facilitate that growth.

I charge you to be patient in the growth of this one and to accept the great gifts as well as the imperfections.

I charge you to use the gifts of this one and cultivate them that they might be used at the optimum level.

I charge you to pray for this one and for his/her family.

I charge you to create opportunities and share the gifts of this preacher for the purpose of Kingdom growth within this congregation and community.

I charge you to bless him/her in such a way that the Lord will be pleased with the way you have honored Him through your treatment of His child and bless you with more sons and daughters to cultivate and send out to His glory.

I CHARGE YOU!

# APPENDIX VI
## EXAMPLE ORDINATION ORDER OF SERVICE

**Invocation**
The pastor of the ordaining church or another minister may deliver the invocation.

**Hymn**

**Prayer**

.
**Responsive Reading**
Many passages of Scripture are fitting for an ordination. Assemble a series of passages significant to the life and ministry of the candidate. Involving the congregation through a responsive reading allows for greater corporate participation in the service.

**Introduction of the Ordaining Council**
The pastor will introduce those who have made up the training team and the ordaining council. These are also the persons who will sign off on the ordination of the candidate along with the pastor standing as credible and experiential witnesses of candidate's ability and gifting.

**Council Recommendation to the Church**
At this point the council moderator or other council representative reads the formal action taken by the council to recommend that the church proceed in ordaining the candidate.

**Action of the Church on the Recommendation**
The pastor or other church representative asks for formal church action to accept the council's recommendation and ordain the candidate to the gospel ministry.

**Selection**
The candidate may have a particular request for the music performed and the groups or individuals who participate in

the service.

## Charge to the Church
This preacher will primarily advise the church on its responsibilities to the newly ordained man. It has been traditional to have a separate ordination sermon to present the Biblical basis of ordination. If a church chooses not to have this separate sermon, the author delivering the charge to the church could also cover that topic. In cases where the ordained man will not continue to serve at that particular church (such as a missionary or other man being sent forth from the church), a charge to the candidate from the pastor of the ordaining church could be substituted.

## Charge to the Candidate
This sermon provides an occasion for the pastor or one who has been influential in the candidate's life to remind him of the solemn privileges and responsibilities accompanying ordination.

## Laying On of Hands and Ordination Prayer
"The actual act of ordination [in the New Testament] consisted of the laying on of hands. This is in many ways the central moment of the service and the part with the clearest Biblical precedent. The pastor lays the primary hand upon the candidate and then any other pastoral staff members of the church would certainly participate in this part of the service. The invitation will also be extended to other examination council members or ordained men present at the service. The pastor or a designee then prays and asks for God's blessing on the newly ordained person.

## Right Hand of Fellowship/Presentation of Ordination Certificate
The pastor of the ordaining church or a representative minister welcomes the newly ordained person to his role.

## Response from the Candidate
It is appropriate at this point for the newly ordained man to speak a few words of thanks, particularly to the One who put him into service (1 Tim. 1:12).

## Hymn/Benediction

This prayer may be offered by the newly ordained man or the pastor of the ordaining church.

## Closing Hymn

A short hymn of benediction, such as the Doxology, provides an appropriate ending to the service.

# APPENDIX VII
# ORDINATION CATECHISM

*This section is intentionally left blank so that one may ponder the questions without the distraction of the answers. A blended one is in the book with both questions and answers. An extensive study guide for the entire catechism is available.*

## Part I

Are you saved?

How do you know?

How long have you been saved?

Explain the road to salvation

Explain your call to ministry.

What is your spiritual gift(s)?

How long have you been preaching/set aside?

How much time do you spend in prayer per week?

How much time do you spend in study per week?

Are you prepared for this catechism?

Has your pastor been helpful in preparing you?

Can you function as an ordained minister in this church?

What is the mission statement of this church?

What is the vision statement of this church?

How do you feel about each?

What do you feel that ministry really is?

What does ordination mean?

Give both an Old Testament and New Testament example of ordination.

What do you feel that your particular area of ministry is?

What gifts do you feel that you have?

How have you worked to develop these gifts?

What are your strengths and weaknesses in ministry?

What do you believe that this ordination does for you?

Can you quit this service to God?


## Part II

What is your position on the Word of God and its place in the church?

What does the word "bible" mean?

What are four views of the Bible?
1.
2.
3.
4.

What is your view of the bible?

What is our bible?

Define Doctrine

Define Theology

How do we determine doctrine?

How do we determine theology?

What are the main parts of the Bible?

How many writings in the Bible?

How many parts to the Old Testament?

How many parts to the New Testament?

What five sections comprise the Old Testament?

1.
2.
3.
4.
5.

Define Pentateuch

What is the Pentateuch?

What is the Torah?

What are the Historical books?

What are the Poetic books?

What are the Major Prophets?

What are the Minor Prophets?

What is the language of the Old Testament?

What is the language of the New Testament?

What is the Septuagint?

What is the Vulgate? Who wrote it?

What are Pseudipigrapha?

What is Apocrypha?

What does "Jesus" mean?

What are some of the Old Testament Names of God?
(You may be asked to Explain)

# Part III

What is the Virgin Birth?

What is incarnation?

What does "gospel" mean?

What does synoptic mean?

What are the four gospels?

Which ones are synoptic?

What are the Johannine writings?

What are the Petrine Writings?

What are the Lukan writings (writings of Luke)?

What is the N.T. History book?

What are the two most doctrinal N. T. writings?

What is an epistle?

What are the Pauline epistles?

What are the Prison epistles?

What are the Pastoral epistles?

What are the General epistles?

What is the N.T. Apocalypse?

What does apocalypse mean?

Define Inspiration

Who wrote the Bible?

Define Disciple?

Define Preacher

Define Pastor

Define Deacon

What are the three aspects of salvation?

What does repentance mean?

What are the three parts to faith?

What is Justification?

What is Sanctification?

What is Grace?

Who is the Triune God?

Define Homo-ousious

Define Homoi-ousious

Is God Homo-ousious or Homoi-ousious?

Define Only Begotten Son

Who is the Holy Spirit?

What is the Gift of the Holy Spirit?

What does it mean to be born of the Spirit?

What does it mean to walk in the Spirit?

What does it mean to be filled with the Spirit?

What does it mean to resist the Spirit?

What does it mean to quench the Spirit?

What does it mean to grieve the Spirit?

When do you receive the baptism of the Spirit?

What are some of the gifts of the Spirit?

What does it mean to be sealed by the Spirit?

What is Communion/Lord's Supper?

What does the bread represent?
What does the fruit of the vine represent?

What does the table in Communion represent?

What do the white coverings represent?

What do the trays represent?

What does the gold represent?

What does the cross represent?

What do we represent?

What is the literal definition of baptism?

Who should be baptized?

What is the water representative of?

When you go in the water, what are you doing?

When you go down in the water, what are you doing?

Raised out of the water means....

Coming out of the water means...

What is Adoption?

# Part IV

What is Philosophy?

What is Psychology?

What is Sociology?

What is Theology?

What is Christology?

What is Pneumatology?

What is Anthropology?

What is Eschatology?

What is Ecclesiology?

What is the church militant?

What is the church triumphant?

What is Soteriology?

What is Hamartiology?

# Part V

Are you a Protestant or Roman Catholic?

Define Catholic. Explain Roman Catholic.

Explain which one you are.

Why?

What event marked the beginning of Protestantism?

Who is Martin Luther?

Who is King James?

What is the Authorized Version of the Bible?

Who wrote it?

When was it written?

Why are you a Baptist?

IF YOU ARE NOT BAPTIST THIS SECTION MAY VE SUBSTITUTED WITH LIKE QUESTIONS FROM YOUR DENOMINATION.

What is a Baptist?

Give a little history of the Baptist Church.

Where was the first Baptist church organized in the United States?

Who was its organizer?

Why was it organized?

Where was the first black Baptist church organized?

What principals provide the theological framework for the Baptist Church?

What are they?

What is the church covenant?

What type of government does the Baptist Church practice?

What is a Baptist association?

What is a Baptist convention?

Name some of the major Baptist conventions in the USA.

What other Denominations are you aware of in the Christian Church?

What other African American Denominations are you aware of?

What is the five-fold ministry?

Briefly explain each aspect.

What is a deacon?

What are some of the pre-requisites for being a deacon?

Why were the first deacons appointed?

Under what authority do deacons serve?

What is a deaconess?

What is a trustee?

Why do we have trustees in church?

Which has more authority: deacons or trustees?

What is a pastor's job?

What are the pre-requisites for being a pastor?

What is your philosophy of preaching?

How do you arrive at a message?

What five elements ought to be in every sermon?

How many points ought a sermon have?

Define the following:

Expository preaching

Biographical preaching

What is your philosophy of ministry?

In one minute tell us of your Christian life experience

In one minute tell us of your call to preach

What will this ordination mean to you?

What does it say to others?

What does it not mean?

What are the grounds for revoking of an Ordination License?

Can you work with your pastor?

Where does your spouse stand in your ministry?

Can you lead your spouse in ministry?

Do you feel competent to continue on to ordination?

# APPENDIX VIII
## ORDINATION CATECHISM ANSWER KEY

*Part I: This part of the catechism is personal, historical and philosophical. In preparation these questions should be studied and answered for clarity's sake and the candidate should be very comfortable before moving on to the next section.*

Are you saved?
Yes

How do you know?
Because I have received Jesus as my Lord

How long have you been saved?
State the time or year that you received Christ.

Explain the road to salvation
Utilize the Roman's Road Presentation

Explain your call to ministry.
Share your personal story of when, where and how God called you to preach and minister.

What is your spiritual gift(s)?
Identify what it/they are.
Example: Helps; Administration, Teaching etc.

How long have you been preaching/set aside?
Identify your calling date and entry to the preaching ministry

How much time do you spend in prayer per week?
Answer truthfully. There is no right or wrong answer

How much time do you spend in study per week?
Answer truthfully.   There is no right or wrong answer

Are you prepared for this catechism?
Yes

Has your pastor been helpful in preparing you?
State the areas that you have received help from your pastor.
Example: in preaching, teaching, managing my study time etc.

Can you function as an ordained minister in this church?
Yes

What do you feel that ministry really is?
The New Testament says we are commanded to serve one another.
None of the words for service or ministry is restricted to the ordained
clergy. All members are enslaved to one another. We all have
obligations to one another. Whether our service is in word or in
deed, it is our duty. We are all called to serve the Lord by serving
one another.

As slave-servants, we are ministering to one another, to the church,
to the gospel and to the Lord. God has given each of us a ministry.
We should minister to one another's needs. God has given us
abilities so that we will use them to serve others. All Christians –
whether men, women, deacons or elders – are called to be ministers

What does ordination mean?
The word ordain in the Bible refers to a setting in place or
designation; for example

Give Old Testament and New Testament examples of ordination.
Example:   Joseph was "ordained" as a ruler in Egypt (Acts 7:10);
the steward in Jesus' parable was "ordained" to oversee a household
(Matthew 24:45); deacons were "ordained" to serve the Jerusalem
church (Acts 6:1-6); and pastors were "ordained" in each city in

Crete (Titus 1:5). Acts 13 includes a good example of a ministerial appointment: "While they were worshiping the Lord and fasting, the Holy Spirit said, 'Set apart for me Barnabas and Saul for the work to which I have called them.' So after they had fasted and prayed, they placed their hands on them and sent them off. The two of them, sent on their way by the Holy Spirit, went down to Seleucia" (vv. 2-4). In this passage, we note some key facts: 1) It is God Himself who calls the men to the ministry and qualifies them with gifts (Acts 20:28; Ephesians 4:11). 2) The members of the church recognize God's clear leading and embrace it. 3) With prayer and fasting, the church lays hands on Paul and Barnabas to demonstrate their commissioning (cf. Acts 6:6; 1 Timothy 5:22). 4) God works through the church, as both the church and the Spirit are said to "send" the missionaries.

What do you feel that your particular area of ministry is?
Share (Include Preaching and Teaching)

Where do you like and feel called to serve?
Share

What areas of ministry to you currently work in.
Share truthfully

What gifts do you feel that you have?
Share what you know and what you feel you may be entering.

Identify what you know you have been gifted to do by God relating to the Kingdom.
Share openly

How have you worked to develop these gifts?
Share your efforts, experience and education

Explain your discipline and learning experiences in your gifting area.
Share any formal as well as informal training that you may get.

What are your strengths and weaknesses in ministry?

Be honest about what your strengths and identify the places where you feel you need to be stronger.

What do you believe that this ordination does for you?

What do you feel you become by being ordained?
Personal

What authority to you feel you received?
Explain

What do you feel you may do not that you could not do before?
Personal consideration here.

Can you quit this service to God?
The answer here should be "no" if you are committed to this ministry.

# Part II

What are the eighteen articles of faith?
They are the fundamental teaching of the Baptist Church

Name Nine of them

## 1. Of the Scriptures

We believe that the Holy Bible was written by men divinely inspired, and is a perfect treasure of heavenly instruction: that it has God for its author, salvation for its end, and truth without any mixture of error, for its matter; that it reveals the principles by which God will judge us; and therefore is, and shall remain to the end of the world, the true center of Christian union, and the supreme standard by which all human conduct, creeds, and opinions should be tried.

## 2. Of the True God

We believe that there is one, and only one, living and true God, an infinite, intelligent Spirit, whose name is JEHOVAH, the Maker and Supreme Ruler of heaven and earth; inexpressibly glorious in holiness, and worthy of all possible honor, confidence, and love; that in the unity of the Godhead there are three persons, the Father, the Son, and the Holy Ghost; equal in divine perfection, and executing distinct but harmonious offices in the great work of redemption.

## 3. Of the Fall of Man

We believe that man was created in holiness, under the law of his Maker; but by voluntary transgression fell from that holy and happy state; in consequence of which all mankind are now sinners, not by constraint, but choice; being by nature utterly void of that holiness required by the law of God, positively inclined to evil; and therefore under just condemnation to eternal ruin, without defense or excuse.

## 4. Of the Way of Salvation

We believe that the salvation of sinners is wholly of grace; through the mediatorial offices of the Son of God; who by the appointment of the Father, freely took upon him our nature, yet without sin; honored the divine law by his personal obedience, and by his death made atonement for our sins; that having risen from the dead he is now enthroned in heaven; and uniting in his wonderful person the tenderest sympathies with divine perfections, he is every way qualified to be a suitable, a compassionate, and an all-sufficient Savior.

## 5. Of Justification

We believe that the great gospel blessing which Christ secures to such as believe in him is Justification; that Justification includes the pardon of sin, and the promise of eternal life on principles of righteousness; that it is bestowed, not in consideration of any works of righteousness which we have done, but solely through faith in the

Redeemer's blood; by virtue of which faith his perfect righteousness is freely imputed to us of God; that it brings us into a state of most blessed peace and favor with God, and secures every other blessing needful for time and eternity.

## 6. <u>Of the Freeness of Salvation</u>

We believe that the blessings of salvation are made free to all by the gospel; that it is the immediate duty of all to accept them by a cordial, penitent, and obedient faith; and that nothing prevents the salvation of the greatest sinner on earth but his own inherent depravity and voluntary rejection of the gospel; which rejection involves him in an aggravated condemnation.

## 7. <u>Of Grace in Regeneration</u>

We believe that, in order to be saved, sinners must be regenerated or born again; that regeneration consists in giving a holy disposition to the mind; that it is effected, in a manner above our comprehension, by the power of the Holy Spirit in connection with divine truth, so as to secure our voluntary obedience to the gospel; and that is proper evidence appears in the holy fruits of repentance and faith and newness of life.

## 8. <u>Of Repentance and Faith</u>

We believe that Repentance and Faith are sacred duties, and also inseparable graces, wrought in our souls by the regenerating Spirit of God; whereby, being deeply convinced of our guilt, danger, and helplessness, and of the way of salvation by Christ, we turn to God with unfeigned contrition, confession and supplication for mercy; at the same time heartily receiving the Lord Jesus Christ as our Prophet, Priest, and King, and relying on him alone as the only and all-sufficient Savior.

## 9. <u>Of God's Purpose of Grace</u>

We believe that Election is the eternal purpose of God, according to which he graciously regenerates, sanctifies, and saves sinners; that being perfectly consistent with the free agency of man, it comprehends all the means in connection with the end; that it is a most glorious display of God's sovereign goodness, being infinitely free, wise, holy, and unchangeable; that it utterly excludes boasting and promotes humility, love, prayer, praise, trust in God, and active imitation of his free mercy; that it encourages the use of means in the highest degree; that it may be ascertained by its effects in all who truly believe the gospel; that it is the foundation of Christian assurance; and that to ascertain it with regard to ourselves demands and deserves the utmost diligence.

Name the next Nine

## 10. Of Sanctification

We believe that Sanctification is the process by which, according to the will of God, we are made partakers of his holiness; that it is a progressive work; that it is begun in regeneration; and that it is carried on in the hearts of believers by the presence and power of the Holy Spirit, the Sealer and Comforter, in the continual use of the appointed means, especially the word of God, self-examination, self-denial, watchfulness, and prayer.

## 11. Of the Perseverance of the Saints

We believe that such only are real believers as endure unto the end; that their persevering attachment to Christ is the grand mark which distinguishes them from superficial professors; that a special Providence watches over their welfare; and that they are kept by the power of God through faith unto salvation.

## 12. Of the Harmony of the Law and the Gospel

We believe that the Law of God is the eternal and unchangeable rule of his moral government; that it is holy, just, and good; and that the inability which the Scriptures ascribe to fallen men love of sin; to deliver them from which, and to restore them through a Mediator to unfeigned obedience to the holy Law, is one great end of the gospel, and of the means of grace connected with the establishment of the visible church.

## 13. Of a Gospel Church

We believe that a visible church of Christ is a congregation of baptized believers, associated by covenant in the faith and fellowship of the gospel; observing the ordinances of Christ; governed by his laws; and exercising the gifts, rights, and privileges invested in them by his rights, and privileges invested in them by his word; that its only Scriptural officers are Bishops, or Pastors, and Deacons, whose qualifications, claims, and duties are defined in the epistles to Timothy and Titus.

## 14. Of Baptism and the Lord's Supper

We believe that Christian Baptism is the immersion in water of a believer, into the name of the Father, and Son, and Holy Ghost; to show forth, in a solemn and beautiful emblem, our faith in the crucified, buried, and risen Savior, with its effect in our death to sin and resurrection to a new life; that it is prerequisite to the privileges of a church relation; and to the Lord's Supper; in which the members of the church, by the sacred use of bread and wine are to commemorate together the dying love of Christ; preceded always by solemn self-examination.

## 15. Of the Christian Sabbath

We believe that the first day of the week is the Lord's Day, or Christian Sabbath; and is to be kept sacred to religious purposes, by abstaining from all secular labor and sinful recreations; by the devout observance of all the means of grace, both private and public; and by preparation for that rest that remains for the people of God.

## 16. Of Civil Government

We believe that civil government is of divine appointment, for the interests and good order of human society; and that magistrates are to be prayed for, conscientiously honored and obeyed; except only in things opposed to the will of our Lord Jesus Christ, who is the only Lord of the conscience, and the Prince of the kings of the earth.

## 17. Of the Righteous and the Wicked

We believe that there is a radical and essential difference between the righteous and the wicked; that such only as through faith are justified in the name of the Lord Jesus, and sanctified by the spirit of our God, are truly righteous in his esteem; while al such as continue in impenitence and unbelief are in his sight wicked, and under the curse; and this distinction holds among men both in and after death.

## 18. Of the World to Come

We believe that the end of the world is approaching; that at the last day Christ will descend from heaven, and raise the dead from the grave to final retribution; that a solemn separation will then take place; that the wicked will be adjudged to endless punishment, and the righteous to endless joy; and that this judgment will fix forever the final state of men in heaven or hell, on principles of righteousness.


What is the Apostles Creed?
The Apostles' Creed, is an early statement of Christian belief—a creed or "symbol". It is widely used by a number of Christian denominations for both liturgical and catechetical purposes, most visibly the Roman Catholic Church, Lutheranism and Anglicanism. It is also used by Presbyterians, Methodists and Congregationalists.

The Text of the Creed
I believe in God the Father Almighty, Maker of heaven and earth.

And in Jesus Christ his only Son our Lord; who was conceived by the Holy Ghost, born of the Virgin Mary, suffered under Pontius Pilate, was crucified, dead, and buried; he descended into hell; the third day he rose again from the dead; he ascended into heaven, and sits on the right hand of God the Father Almighty; from thence he shall come to judge the quick and the dead.

I believe in the Holy Ghost; the holy catholic Church; the communion of saints; the forgiveness of sins; the resurrection of the body; and the life everlasting. AMEN

What is the Nicene Creed?

A formal statement of Christian belief that is widely used in Christian liturgies, based on that adopted at the first Council of Nicaea in 325.

The Text of the Creed

We believe in one God the Father Almighty, Maker of heaven and earth, and of all things visible and invisible. And in one Lord Jesus Christ, the only-begotten Son of God, begotten of the Father before all worlds, God of God, Light of Light, Very God of Very God, begotten, not made, being of one substance with the Father by whom all things were made; who for us men, and for our salvation, came down from heaven, and was incarnate by the Holy Spirit of the Virgin Mary, and was made man, and was crucified also for us under Pontius Pilate. He suffered and was buried, and the third day he rose again according to the Scriptures, and ascended into heaven, and sits on the right hand of the Father. And he shall come again with glory to judge both the quick and the dead, whose kingdom shall have no end.

And we believe in the Holy Spirit, the Lord and Giver of Life, who proceedeth from the Father and the Son, who with the Father and the Son together is worshipped and glorified, who spoke by the prophets. And we believe one holy catholic and apostolic Church.

We acknowledge one baptism for the remission of sins. And we look for the resurrection of the dead, and the life of the world to come. Amen.

What is a Church Covenant?
Any church covenant is simply the stated beliefs and teachings of that particular church.

What is the Baptist Church Covenant?

Having been led, as we believe, by the Spirit of God, to receive the Lord Jesus Christ as our Savior, and on the profession of our faith, having been baptized in the name of the Father, and of the Son, and of the Holy Spirit, we do now in the presence of God and this assembly, most solemnly and joyfully enter into covenant with one another, as one body in Christ.

We engage, therefore, by the aid of the Holy Spirit, to walk together in Christian love; to strive for the advancement of this church in knowledge, holiness, and comfort; to promote its prosperity and spirituality; to sustain its worship, ordinances, discipline, and doctrines; to contribute cheerfully and regularly to the support of the ministry, the expenses of the church, the relief of the poor, and the spread of the Gospel through all nations.

We also engage to maintain family and personal devotion; to religiously educate our children; to seek the salvation of our kindred and acquaintances; to walk circumspectly in the world; to be just in our dealings, faithful in our engagements, and exemplary in our conduct; to avoid all gossip, backbiting, and unrighteous anger; to abstain from all forms of activity which dishonor our Lord Jesus Christ, bring harm to the body which is the Temple of the Holy Spirit, cause stumbling to a fellow believer, or hinder the winning of a soul to Christ; and to be zealous in our efforts to advance the kingdom of our Savior.

We further engage to watch over one another in Christian love; to remember each other in prayer; to aid each other in sickness and distress; to cultivate Christian sympathy in feeling and courtesy in speech; to be slow to take offense, but always ready for reconciliation and mindful of the rules of our Savior, to secure it without delay.

We moreover engage that, when we remove from this place, we will as soon as possible unite with some other church where we can carry out the spirit of this covenant and the principles of God's Word.

What does the word "bible" mean?
It literally means book. (Greek "biblios")

What are four views of the Bible?
The bible is about the Word of God; The bible contains the Word of God; The bible becomes the Word of God as it applies to you; The bible is The Word of God

What is your view of the bible?
The Bible IS the Word of God

What is our bible?
Literally the Word of God

Define Doctrine
Doctrine means teaching

Define Theology
The study of God

What are the main parts of the Bible?
Old Testament & New Testament

How many writings in the Bible?
66

How many parts to the Old Testament?
39

How many parts to the New Testament?
27

What five sections comprise the Old Testament?
Law, History; Poetry; Major Prophets; Minor Prophets

Define Pentateuch
5 (Penta) teuch (books)

What is the Pentateuch?
The first five books of the bible; Law Books

What is the Torah?
The Law

What are the Historical books?
Joshua; Judges; Ruth; I & II Samuel; I & II Kings; I & II Chronicles; Ezra; Esther; Nehemiah

What are the Poetic books?
Job; Psalms; Proverbs; Ecclesiastes; Song of Solomon

What are the Major Prophets?
Isaiah; Jeremiah; Lamentations; Ezekiel; Daniel

What are the Minor Prophets?
Hosea; Joel; Amos; Obadiah; Jonah; Micah; Nahum; Habakkuk; Zephaniah; Zephaniah; Haggai; Zechariah; Malachi

What is the language of the Old Testament?
Hebrew

What is the language of the New Testament?
Greek

What is the Septuagint?
The Greek version of the Old Testament

What is the Vulgate? Who wrote it?
The Latin Version of the Bible
Jerome

What is Pseudipigrapha?
False (Pseudo) Writings (Grapha)

What is Apocrypha?
It literally means hidden. They are those writings that contained hidden messages that the Jews could recognize during the exile.

What does "Jesus" mean?
Jehovah-Saves; It is the N.T. word for Joshua

Share at least 5 names of God in the Old Testament
(Be Prepared to elaborate on these if asked)

ELOHIM: Genesis 1:1, Psalm 19:1
 meaning "God", a reference to God's power and might.

ADONAI: Malachi 1:6
 meaning "Lord", a reference to the Lordship of God.

JEHOVAH–YAHWEH: Genesis 2:4
 a reference to God's divine salvation.

JEHOVAH-MACCADDESHEH: Exodus 31:13
 meaning "The Lord thy sanctifier"

JEHOVAH-ROHI: Psalm 23:1
 meaning "The Lord my shepherd"

JEHOVAH-SHAMMAH: Ezekiel 48:35
 meaning "The Lord who is present"

JEHOVAH-RAPHA: Exodus 15:26
 meaning "The Lord our healer"

JEHOVAH-TSIDKENU: Jeremiah 23:6
meaning "The Lord our righteousness"

JEHOVAH-JIREH: Genesis 22:13-14
meaning "The Lord will provide"

JEHOVAH-NISSI: Exodus 17:15
meaning "The Lord our banner"

JEHOVAH-SHALOM: Judges 6:24
meaning "The Lord is peace"

JEHOVAH-SABBAOTH: Isaiah 6:1-3
meaning "The Lord of Hosts"

EL-ELYON: Genesis 14:17-20, Isaiah 14:13-14
meaning "The highest God"

EL-ROI: Genesis 16:13
meaning "The strong one who sees"

EL-SHADDAI: Genesis 17:1, Psalm 91:1
meaning "The God of the mountains or God Almighty"

EL-OLAM: Isaiah 40:28-31
meaning "The everlasting God"


# Part III

What does "Christ" mean?
Anointed One

What is the Virgin Birth?
The conception and subsequent bringing forth
of Jesus by Mary without human aid. Jesus literally is the Son of
God

What is incarnation?
The Word became flesh/human

What does "gospel" mean?
Good News

What does synoptic mean?
Similar

What are the four gospels?
Matthew; Mark; Luke; John

Which ones are synoptic?
Matthew; Mark; Luke

What are the Johannine writings?
Gospel of John; I, II, III John; Revelation

What are the Petrine Writings?
I & II Peter

What are the Lukan writings (writings of Luke)?
Gospel of Luke & Acts

What is the N.T. History book?
Acts

What are the two most doctrinal N. T. writings?
Romans and Hebrews

What is an epistle?
A letter

What are the Pauline epistles?
Romans; I & II Corinthians; Galatians; Ephesians; Colossians;
Philippians; I & II Thessalonians; Philemon; I & II Timothy; Titus

---

What are the Prison epistles?
Galatians; Ephesians; Colossians; Philippians; Philemon

What are the Pastoral epistles?
I & II Timothy; Titus

What are the General epistles?
Hebrews; James; I & II Peter; I, II, III John; Jude

What is the N.T. Apocalypse?
Revelation

What does apocalypse mean?

Define Inspiration
God-breathed

Who wrote the Bible?
Holy men inspired by God

Define Disciple?
Disciplined one; follower of Jesus

Define Preacher
Proclaimer/herald of the Gospel

Define Pastor
Shepherd of God's sheep; flock; people

What is the difference between pastoral gifts and pastoral position?
Elaborate

Define Deacon
One who ministers (Greek...diakonos)

What are the three aspects of salvation?
Saved from penalty of Sin
Saved from power of Sin

Saved from presence of Sin

What does repentance mean?
To turn away from…. (literally to turn from Sin)

What are the three parts to faith?
Knowledge (What is known through scripture);
Assent (declaring that what is known is also true)
Trust (confidence in what you know   and give assent to)

What is Justification?
To be declared legally righteous in the sight of God by virtue of the blood of Christ

What is Sanctification?
To be set aside for the purpose of God.  It has two primary aspects 1) Positional: this is what God gives to us at the time of salvation 2) Progressive: the work that the Holy Spirit does daily in the life of the believer.

What is Grace?
The undeserved love and mercy that God shows toward us in-spite of ourselves

Who is the Triune God?
Father; Son; Holy Spirit

Define Homo-ousious
One Substance

Define Homoi-ousious
Of two or more substances

Is God Homo-ousious or Homoi-ousious?
Homo-ousious

Define Only Begotten Son
One and Only Unique Son

Who is the Holy Spirit?
3rd person in the Godhead; Power of God; Comforter; Counselor; Giver of Spiritual gifts

What is the Gift of the Holy Spirit?
The Holy Spirit himself

What does it mean to be born of the Spirit?
To be given new life/ It's a bringing into the body of Christ

What does it mean to walk in the Spirit?
To literally follow him (It's a phrase devised from military meaning to keep in step)

What does it mean to be filled with the Spirit?
To come under the Spirit's control
What does it mean to resist the Spirit?
To set oneself against as an enemy

What does it mean to quench the Spirit?
To put the Spirit's flame out in your life

What does it mean to grieve the Spirit?
To make the Spirit sad by sin

What are some of the gifts of the Spirit?
See Romans 12 & I Corinthians 12

What does it mean to be sealed by the Spirit?
It literally means that God has placed his royal signature/approval on you. You are sealed/secured unto the day of redemption

What is Dynamic Monarchianism?
Dynamic Monarchianism teaches that God is the Father, that Jesus is only a man, denied the personal subsistence of the Logos, and taught that the Holy Spirit was a force or presence of God the Father. Present-

day groups in this category are the Jehovah's Witnesses, Christadelphians, and Unitarians. Additionally, some ancient dynamic monarchianists were also known as Adoptionists who taught that Jesus was tested by God; and after passing this test and upon His baptism, He was granted supernatural powers by God and adopted as the Son. Ancient teachers of dynamic Monarchianism were Theodotians, a Tanner in Byzantium around 190 A.D., and Paul of Samosata a bishop of Antioch in Syria around A.D. 260.


What is Communion/Lord's Supper?
It is the fellowship of believers commemorating/proclaiming the, death, burial, resurrection, ascension and coming again of Our Lord Jesus Christ

What does the bread represent?
His body

What does the fruit of the vine represent?
Shed blood

What does the table in Communion represent?
Fellowship

What do the white coverings represent?
Purity/holiness

What do the trays represent?
Service

What does the gold represent?
Precious/priceless

What does the cross represent?
Christ's

What do we represent?
The priesthood of believers

What is the literal definition of baptism?
It literally means to cause to perish

Who should be baptized?
Believers only

What is the water representative of?
Grave

When you go in the water, what are you doing?
Presenting yourself

When you go down in the water, what are you doing?
That's death

Raised out of the water means....
Resurrection

Coming out of the water means...
Entering a new life

What is Adoption?
To be legally and legitimately brought into the family of God by
God. Made an heir (son or daughter)


# Part IV

What is philosophy?
Love of Wisdom

What is psychology?
Study of the Mind

What is Sociology?
The study of societies

What is theology?

The study of God

What is Christology?
The study of Christ

What is Pneumatology?
The study of the Spirit

What is Anthropology?
The study of man

What is eschatology?
The study of last/coming things

What is Ecclesiology?
The study of the church

What is the church militant?
The church on earth

What is the church triumphant?
The church in glory that have gone on

What is Soteriology?
The study of salvation

What is Hamartiology?
The study of sin

# Part V

Are you a Protestant or Roman Catholic?
Protestant

Define Catholic; Define Roman Catholic
Universal

Explain which one you are.
Protestant

Why?
Historical/Personal explanation

What event marked the beginning of Protestantism?
Martin Luther nailing 95 Theses on the door of the Church at Wittenberg

Who is Martin Luther?
The father of the Reformation; He wrote the 95 Theses; A former Monk; Theologian; Priest

Who is King James?
A 16th Century King of England. He is the King who commissioned the King James Version of the Bible.

What is the Authorized Version of the Bible?
King James Version

Who wrote it?
Forty-seven men appointed for the writing of it are known to have engaged in it. These were divided into six companies, two of which met at Oxford, two at Cambridge, and two at Westminster. They were presided over severally by the Dean of Westminster and by the two Hebrew Professors of the Universities. To the first company, at Westminster (ten in number), was assigned the Old Testament as far as 2 Kings; the second company (seven in number) had the Epistles. The first company at Cambridge (numbering eight) had 2 Chronicles to Ecclesiastes; the second company (numbering seven) had the Apocryphal books. To the first Oxford company (seven in number) were assigned the prophetical books, from Isaiah to Malachi; to the second (eight in number) were given the four Gospels, the Acts and the Apocalypse, or Revelation.

When was it written?
The King James Version, also known as the Authorized Version or

the King James Bible, is an English translation of the Christian Bible for the Church of England begun in 1604 and completed in 1611.

Why are you a Baptist?
Explain your personal reason

What is a Baptist?
Baptists are individuals who comprise a group of Christian denominations and churches that subscribe to a doctrine that baptism should be performed only for professing believers, and that it must be done by complete immersion. Other tenets of Baptist churches include soul competency, salvation through faith alone, Scripture alone as the rule of faith and practice, and the autonomy of the local congregation. Baptists recognize two ministerial offices, elders and deacons. Baptist churches are widely considered to be Protestant churches, though some Baptists disavow this identity.

Give a little history of the Baptist Church.
The first known Baptist Congregation was formed by a number of these fleeing separatists in Amsterdam, Holland in 1608.

It was largely made up of British persons led by John Smyth who along with Thomas Helwys, sought to set up the group according to New Testament patterns.

As they saw it, it was important to 'reconstitute' and not just 'reform' the Church. There was emphasis placed on personal conversion and on baptism, which was to be given to individuals who had personally professed faith in Jesus Christ, that is, to believers only and on mutual covenanting between and among believers.

Some affiliated groups started when members of the Amsterdam group went back to Britain and took the name 'Baptist' to identify themselves. This had to do with the distinctive approach to the meaning and mode of baptism. —*William Cathcart, Baptist Historian/Author*

Where was the first Baptist church organized in the United States?

Providence Rhode Island

Who was its organizer?
Roger Williams in 1638

Where was the first black Baptist church organized?
It is debated. Many attribute it to be First Baptist Church in Savannah, Georgia. Others say that it is First Bryan Church in Savannah, Georgia and others argue that it is Silver Bluff Baptist Church in Beech Island, South Carolina.

What type of government does the Baptist Church practice?
Congregational

What is a Baptist association?
An association is a group of Baptist Churches who voluntarily cooperate together to do, by combined action, what no church could do by itself.

Name some of the major Baptist conventions in the USA.
National Baptist USA Inc., National Baptist of America;
Progressive National Baptists, American Baptists; Southern Baptist;
Full Gospel Baptists

Name some of the Other Mainline Denominations
Episcopal
United Methodist
Presbyterian
Church of Christ
Church of God
Reformed
Lutheran
Assemblies of God

What are some other Mainline African American Denominations?
African Methodist Episcopal
Christian Methodist Episcopal
African Methodist Episcopal Zion

Church of God in Christ
Pentecostal Assemblies of the World

What is the five-fold ministry?
Apostles, Prophets, Pastor-Teachers, Evangelists

Briefly explain each aspect.
Elaborate

What is a deacon?
One who ministers; One of the 2 scriptural Offices
What are some of the pre-requisites for being a deacon?

Why were the first deacons appointed?
To resolve conflict over the distribution of food between Greeks and Hebrews over who their widows were being attended to.

Under what authority do deacons serve?
Pastoral/Church Authority

## What is a deaconess?
A deaconess is a lady who performs the ministry tasks of a deacon except she does so most often to women and children. She ministers with deacons when the occasions call for it.

What is a trustee?
Generally speaking, a church trustee is a layman who takes care of the secular business of running a church. Trustees manage finances and property, and ensure the church is compliant with any legal requirements.

The role of trustee varies depending on denomination and congregation. Trustees may be responsible for maintaining buildings and facilities, tracking the church's equipment and investments, keeping insurance policies up to date, and managing funds. In a large church, a trustee may oversee several different ministries, including a finance department and janitorial staff. In others, the trustee is the janitor. Trustees can be appointed or elected, are occasionally elders or deacons, and may have the authority to serve as signatories for the church. In addition to denominational and congregational requirements, each state has different laws regarding trustees. In some states, churches are required to have trustees.

The position of "trustee" is not a biblically mandated office; rather, it is a practicality to aid the appropriation, maintenance, and disposition of church property. Although trustees are not mentioned in the Bible, their role is biblically appropriate. The New Testament calls us to be good stewards of our blessings, to maintain order in the church, and to use our gifts to benefit the body. I Peter 4:10 says of individuals, "As each one has received a special gift, employ it in serving one another as good stewards of the manifold grace of God." This applies to churches as well.

Which has more authority: deacons or trustees?
Neither...the have unique but different obligations.

What is a pastor's job?
To oversee the people of God. To shepherd or lead. To feed the word of God and administer it to the daily lives of people in whatever needs arise.

What are the pre-requisites for being a pastor?
Saved
Called
Licensed
Ordained
Able to teach
Husband of one wife
Not greedy

Temperate
Not a novice
Not a brawler
Patient

What is your philosophy of preaching?
Express yours in a paragraph or 1minute statement

How do you arrive at a message?
Prayer, Study, Mediation, Inquiring of God

What five elements ought to be in every sermon?
1. Story
2. Call to action
3. Anointing
4. Bible
5. Clarity

Name five different types of preaching
1. Textual
This is an analysis of a specific Scripture text for use in a word for word study.

2. Expository
A comprehensive analysis of larger blocks of Scripture so that the bigger picture can be understood.

3. Topical
A sermon based upon events in the church calendar or on world events, but must remain faithful to God's word.

4. Devotional
Inspirational thoughts on practical issues in a down to earth fashion.

5. Allegorical
Making use of fiction or symbols as a springboard to the understanding of Scripture.
What is Expository Preaching?

It is a form of preaching that details the meaning of a particular text or passage of Scripture. It explains what the Bible means by what it says. Exegesis is technical and grammatical exposition, a careful drawing out of the exact meaning of a passage in its original context.

What is Biographical Preaching
A simple definition is that Biographical preaching is preaching that provides a biography of the life of a person from scripture and draws a moral lesson or message from that story.

What is your philosophy of ministry?
Personal

In one minute tell us of your Christian life experience
Write this out and rehearse it.

In one minute tell us of your call to preach
Write this out and rehearse it

What will this ordination mean to you?
Personal Explanation. Write and rehearse

What does it say to others?
It says that I have sat under the tutoring and training of my pastor and others to learn and meet the requirements for ordination. It suggests a commitment to God, my pastor, this church and community to represent and serve God in the word and in the way.

What does it not mean?
It does not mean that I am free from responsibility and free to do whatever I desire without accountability or

What are the grounds for revoking of an Ordination License?

Can you work with your pastor?
Yes

Where does your spouse stand in your ministry?

My spouse supports me and we have agreed to work together.

Can you lead your spouse in ministry?
Yes. My spouse has agreed to work with me in the capacities that I have been called to and that have been assigned to me by my pastor and church. We have agreed to communicate, pray and work together in every assignment.

Do you feel competent to continue on to ordination?
Yes

# GETTING YOUR THINGS TOGETHER

There are things that a pastor/preacher needs to be able to handle before he/she ever has to handle them. There is a need to be able to put together a variety of them in a way that makes them both confident and successful in them. A few are incorporated here to give you a head start.

# PASTOR
## SPECIAL DAY PLANNING SHEET

The Occasion:

Date:                    Time:                    Location:

The Objective:

The Theme:                    The Scripture Base:

The Speaker:

Why this Speaker?

How does this day glorify God?

The Budget:

How it will be disbursed
1. Speaker(S)
2. Setting
3. Musicians/Vocalists
4. Food
5. Instruments/Equipment
6. Technical Services
7. Supplies: CD'S, DVD's Labels; Print Costs
8. Books/Workbooks
9. Advertising
10. Misc.
Total:

Committee: _____

_____

_____

_____

_____

Chairperson: _____

Co-Chairperson: _____

       Approved _____       Disapproved _____

Pastor Signature: _____

# PASTOR
# REVIVAL PLANNING SHEET

Date:

Time:

Location:

The Objectives:

1.

2.

3.

The Theme:                    The Scripture Base:

Mission:

Prayer Team:

Worship Team:

Outreach Team:

Planning Team:

Finance and Oversight Team:

Social Media Team:

Food and Refreshments:

Media Team:

Hospitality Team:

Transportation Team:

Setup/Custodial Team

The Speaker:                    Why this Speaker?

Transportation for Speaker:

Housing for Speaker:

Biography of Speaker:

---

Restrictions:

Allowances for Spouse:       Yes _____   No _____

Special Needs:

Honorarium

Miscellaneous Considerations _____
_____
_____
_____

Total Budget

Committee _____

_____

_____

_____

Committee Chairperson _____

Committee Co-Chairperson _____

Approved _____    Disapproved _____

Pastor's Signature _____

# PASTOR
## VISITATION PLANNING

Name:

Address:

Type: () Home () Hospital () Nursing Home () Other

Contact Number:

Contact Person:

Condition: () Excellent () Good () Fair () Comatose

Phone Contact:

Prayer Contact:

Operation or Confinement Situation:

Type of Visit: () Phone () Card () In Person

Person(s) Visiting: () Pastor () Pastoral Staff () Deacons
() Deaconesses () Benevolent Committee () Mission Group

Member Needs:

Date (s) Planned:

# PASTOR
## MARRIAGE/WEDDING PLANNING

Bride:                          Groom:


Counseling
Appointments:        Date:                Time:

1.
2.
3.
4.
5.
6.

Counselor:

## Wedding Party

Groom:                                          Bride:

Wedding Coordinator:

Officiant (s)


Best Man:

Maid of Honor:


Matron of Honor:

Groomsmen: _____

_____

_____

_____

_____

Bridesmaids _____

_____

_____

_____

_____

Ushers _____

_____

_____

_____

Parents of the Groom:

Parents of the Bride:

Flower Girl(s) _____

_____

_____

Ring Bearer(s) _____

_____

_____

Musicians/Soloists _____

_____

_____

_____

_____

Florist:

Photographer:

Videographer:

Caterer:

Limousine Service

Location of Wedding Rehearsal:
Time:

Location of Rehearsal Dinner:
Time:

Location of Wedding:
Time:

Location of Reception:
Time:

Special Requests

# PASTOR
## FUNERAL PLANNING SHEET

Date of Death:

Location of Death:

Family Residence:

Contact Person:

First Visitation:
1. Consolation
2. Confrontation
3. Celebration

Second Visitation:
1. Assignment to Deacons/Deaconesses
2. Secure Funeral Home Information
3. Schedule Date and Time
4. Type of Service (Memorial or Funeral)
5. Location of Funeral
6. Arrival time at church for body
7. Open casket or closed cast funeral?
8. Will there be a Wake?
9. If so, when and where

## OBITUARY INFORMATION:

The Honoree:

Born:

Raised:

Educated:

Accepted Christ:

Profession:

Marriage:

Parents:

Siblings:

Children:

Grandchildren:

Hobbies:

Memberships and Affiliations:

Accomplishments:

## THE PROGRAM

Officiant (s)

Musicians:

Choir:

Ushers:

Eulogist:

Pulpit Assistance:

Testimonials (3 Minutes)

Clerk:

Requested Music: _____

_____

_____

_____

Honorary Pall Bearers _____

_____

_____

_____

_____

_____

Active Pall Bearers _____

_____

_____

_____

_____

Flower Attendants _____

_____

_____

_____

Interment:

Repass:

# PASTORAL FOLLOW-UP

## Notes

One Week follow-up:

One Month Follow-up

# PASTOR
## SALARY NEGOTIATION PLAN SHEET

Base Salary:

Life Insurance:

Health Insurance:

Retirement:

Travel Allowance:

Workmen's Compensation:

Housing Allowance
1. Rent
2. Utilities
3. Phone

Vacation:

Conferences and Conventions:
1.
2.
3.
4.

Continuing Education:

Book Allowance:

# PASTOR
## BIOGRAPHICAL SKETCH INFORMATION

## PERSONAL

Name

Birthdate:

Place of Birth:

Parents:

Spouse:

Children:

## EDUCATION

1. Grade School:

2. College or Trade School:

3. Graduate School:

4. Other Professional Training:

## MINISTRY EXPERIENCE

Licensed to Preach:
By:
Where:
When:

Ordained to Preach:
By:
Where:
When:


MINISTRY POSITIONS HELD:

Position:

Where:

Dates


Position:

Where:

Dates


Position:

Where:

Dates


Position:

Where:

Dates

HOBBIES


AFFILIATIONS


WRITINGS


SPECIAL RECOGNITIONS/HONORS


REFERENCES

**Professional**

1.
Name
Address
Phone
Company

Relationship

2.
Name
Address
Phone
Company
Relationship

3.
Name
Address
Phone
Company
Relationship

4.
Name
Address
Phone
Company
Relationship

**Personal:**

1.
Name
Address
Phone
Relationship

2.
Name
Address
Phone

Relationship

3.
Name
Address
Phone
Relationship

4.
Name
Address
Phone
Relationship


EDUCATION

1. Grade School:
   Location:
   Years Attended:
   Graduated:

2. College or Trade School:
   Location:
   Years Attended:
   Graduated:

3. Graduate School:
   Location:
   Years Attended:
   Graduated:


3. Other Professional Training:
   Location:
   Years Attended:
   Graduated:

# WORKS BY VERNON LLOYD

Mirrors, Windows and Doors

A Cord of Three Strands: Exceptional Evangelism

So You Want to Be a Preacher: Tutoring Trainees for Ministry

So You Call Yourself a Preacher Training Manual

Men of Honor Training Course